DOG GROOMING

for Beginners

Quarto.com

© 2023 Quarto Publishing Group USA Inc.
Text © 2014Jorge Bendersky
Photography © 2014 Quarry Books

First Published in 2023 by New Shoe Press, an imprint of The Quarto Group,
100 Cummings Center, Suite 265-D, Beverly, MA 01915, USA.
T (978) 282-9590 F (978) 283-2742

Essential, In-Demand Topics, Four-Color Design, Affordable Price
New Shoe Press publishes affordable, beautifully designed books covering evergreen, in-demand subjects. With a goal to inform and inspire readers' everyday hobbies, from cooking and gardening to wellness and health to art and crafts, New Shoe titles offer the ultimate library of purposeful, how-to guidance aimed at meeting the unique needs of each reader. Reimagined and redesigned from Quarto's best-selling backlist, New Shoe books provide practical knowledge and opportunities for all DIY enthusiasts to enrich and enjoy their lives.

Visit Quarto.com/New-Shoe-Press for a complete listing of the New Show Press books.

New Shoe Press titles are also available at discount for retail, wholesale, promotional, and bulk purchase. For details, contact the Special Sales Manager by email at specialsales@quarto.com or by mail at The Quarto Group, Attn: Special Sales Manager, 100 Cummings Center, Suite 265-D, Beverly, MA 01915, USA.

2

ISBN: 978-0-7603-8396-4
eISBN: 978-0-7603-8397-1

The content in this book was previously published in *DIY Dog Grooming* (Quarry Books 2014) by Jorge Bendersky.

Library of Congress Cataloging-in-Publication Data available

Cover Images: Marshall Boprey
Hair and Makeup: Dominic Pucciarello
Photography: Marshall Boprey, except pages 15-20, 25, 26, 30, 33, 45, 70, 126, 128, 134-135 (Shutterstock.com); and as otherwise indicated.

Printed in China

DOG GROOMING

for Beginners

JORGE BENDERSKY

Simple Techniques for Washing, Trimming, Cleaning & Clipping All Breeds of Dogs

N

NEW SHOE PRESS

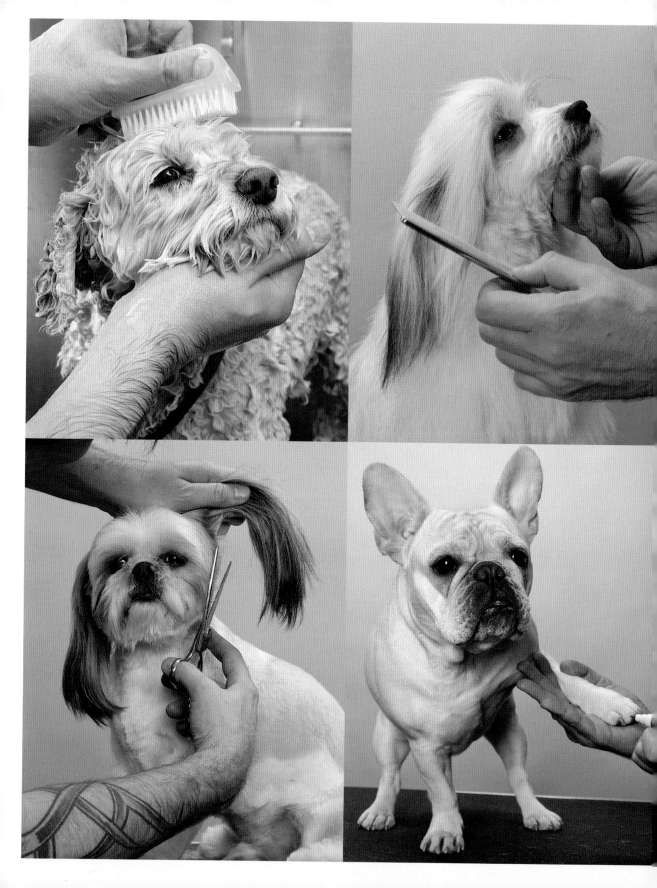

Contents

Foreword

Many dog lovers I know take responsible care of their pets and think they have everything covered—exercise, training, food and water, and regular visits to the vet. But one very important area that is easy for people to forget is grooming, especially if they have a nonshedding breed with shorter fur or a hypoallergenic dog with hair.

There are many reasons grooming your dog regularly is important. Change of climate may seem obvious, with dogs needing shorter cuts in summer and longer cuts but more frequent brushing in winter. But there are other reasons to groom your dog. Avoiding or removing matted hair or burrs is one example. Another important reason is that proper grooming is a vital part of flea and tick control.

Finally, because the grooming process involves close contact with your entire dog, it is a great way to detect skin problems, rashes, bumps, or other issues early on, when they are more easily—and more cheaply—treatable.

Despite all these important reasons, though, a lot of people do not get their dogs professionally groomed often enough, if at all. Maybe there aren't any professional groomers located conveniently, or their dog may have fear or aggression issues that prevent them from being groomed. And, of course, there are always valid economic reasons. Some people just may not be able to afford a professional groomer.

If you learn how to properly bathe and groom your dog yourself, though, all of those reasons not to do it will disappear. You can groom your dog at home, on your schedule. Ideally, your dog won't be afraid if it's you doing it, and once you have your grooming tools and supplies together, the expense of grooming your own dogs is minimal.

Of course, you also need a good teacher to show you how to do it, and in putting together this do-it-yourself guide, Jorge Bendersky, one of Manhattan's most sought-after dog groomers, shares his years of expertise and love of teaching with you.

I've met Jorge many times, particularly in connection with his rescue work through North Shore Animal League America, and he has the same instinctual approach to dogs that I do. In fact, we both describe working with dogs the same way, as a dance—a partnership with a leader and a follower, built on trust. Like dance, working with our dogs involves consistency, practice, and learning in small steps. Most of all, though, it's a lot of fun.

I can tell when watching Jorge do what he does that it isn't a job for him. It's fun, it's a dance, and it's joyful. I feel the same way when I "work" with dogs. He has also mastered the ability to project calm, assertive energy, which comes through in the pages of this book.

While you can make excuses not to take your dog to the groomer, you have no reason to make excuses for not doing it yourself any longer. *DIY Dog Grooming, From Puppy Cuts to Best in Show* is a comprehensive guide that covers the basics of hair, nail, ear, and paw care, as well as grooming styles and techniques, but Jorge doesn't stop with the basics. He covers the tools of the trade and how to bathe your dog and also includes simple grooming solutions that you probably already have in your kitchen cabinet. He also covers solutions to common dog problems that you wouldn't think about until you need to deal with them, like gum in the fur, fleas and ticks, and even what to do if your dog meets the wrong end of a skunk.

My fans know about my "Exercise, Discipline, and then Affection, in that order" fulfillment formula, but they often can't think of ways to show affection beyond food, treats, and petting. Grooming your dogs yourself is an incredible way to show affection while strengthening your bond and building trust with your dogs. Trust Jorge and he'll show you how to groom your dogs right.

— Cesar Millan
  June 2013

Editor's Note: This Foreword appeared in the unabridged version of this book,
DIY Dog Grooming, From Puppy Cuts to Best in Show
(Quarry Books 2014)

Introduction

The Tango Theory

In an ideal world, given the right information and experience, nobody would be able to groom your dog better than you. There will always be benefits to taking your dog to a professional groomer, but no matter how professional and caring your groomer is, he or she will never share that same special bond that you do with your best friend—your dog.

Let me be clear. This is not only a book about saving money, but it's also a book that will improve both you and your dog's quality of life. Taking the time and effort to learn how to groom your dog is a beautiful learning experience that will teach you new and wonderful things about your dog, and you will discover that the more you learn about your dog, the better dog owner you will become. Your dog loves and trusts you more than anyone else and will appreciate being groomed by you more than by someone else.

Another bonus is that by adding some extra steps to your regular routine with your dog, you will stretch the time between visits to the groomer and therefore save money. Also, when you are away from home, knowing the basics of grooming will help you avoid paying high prices for last-minute grooming appointments.

A simple day running around outside at the park or even at the beach or the pool can not only turn a dog's fashion statement into a fashion nightmare, but also expose him to possible health issues including small cuts, rashes, fleas, and ticks. The best way to keep these problems from getting worse is by detecting them early, and the easiest way to recognize them early is when you are properly grooming or brushing a dog yourself. Additionally, many serious health issues are first noticed during grooming. Catching and addressing them early on can save a dog's life and you a lot of money.

I have often said that grooming your dog is like dancing a tango. You and your dog can do this grooming dance together and create your own sparkle. I will show you the steps. It's a dance that, when done together, will enhance that special relationship you already have.

CHAPTER 1

Identification

When grooming, the first thing you must do is to correctly identify what type of coat your dog has. This will determine what products you need to buy and even what techniques you should most focus on mastering.

Familiarizing yourself with as many aspects of a particular breed as possible, and trying to anticipate what a certain breed's needs could be, will give you an approximate idea of how much time and money you will spend for the next sixteen years or so in caring for your best friend. Some of the saddest stories are those of dogs that are poorly cared for due to a lack of funds or, even worse, of people who must surrender their pets because they simply cannot afford to take care of them.

It is also never too late to learn new information. Learning about the grooming needs of a dog that you already have in your home, or learning about the latest grooming developments regarding the breed you already have, will allow you to buy better tools that will not only make your next grooming job easier but make your dog's next grooming experience a happier one.

Identifying Your Dog

With more than four hundred recognized breeds around the world and with so many breed mixes, we can find lots of different hair type combinations.

We can start by dividing them into three big categories:
- Straight Hair
- Curly Hair
- Wiry Hair

Within these three big groups, we can find three different lengths:
- Short
- Medium
- Long

And most of them can be divided into two subcategories:
- Double Coated (dogs with undercoat)
- Single Coated

To all this, we can still add more divisions based on how low or high maintenance the grooming requirements will be.

Purebreds

The benefits of having a purebred dog is that we can have a more certain idea of how the dog's coat will evolve. Over years and even centuries of responsible breeding, purebred dogs have been "engineered" to carry on certain characteristics that are now embedded in their genetic makeup. Therefore, we can for the most part expect the kind of coat our dog will have, their temperament, and the kind of activity they will require to stay in shape. This also makes it easier for us to learn and prepare for what we are getting into when we welcome a specific breed into our home.

Mixed Breeds

When adopting a mixed-breed dog, there is no long established reservoir of information to give any indication of the kind of coat, grooming requirements, and temperament he will have. As they get older, most puppies will start changing their puppy coats on their backs, starting at the base of the tail and moving forward to the neck as they grow. If it is a terrier mix, the coat will follow the terrier genetic trait; the coat on the back, near the tail, will be the first area that will grow in harsh and wavy. If the dog has a drop coat, as the puppy loses his puppy coat (which is usually fluffy and woolly), the adult coat will grow in straight and shiny.

High Maintenance

Let us start by acknowledging that every dog is high maintenance with regards to all the attention he will need to be properly taken care of, but the degree of maintenance will depend on the breed. There is no doubt that a Weimaraner will have much fewer grooming requirements than an Old English sheepdog or a Pekingese. Although the length of the coat is not the only factor that will determine the level of grooming attention they will need, it is a major one.

Some dogs with short or medium-length coats could shed a lot, making them very high maintenance. A long-haired dog that only sheds seasonally or that barely sheds at all will still require a good grooming routine but much less vacuuming around the house.

Low Maintenance

Obviously, dogs with very short hair with no undercoat, such as a Weimaraner, a miniature pinscher, or an Italian greyhound, are very low maintenance when it comes to grooming because they barely shed or don't shed at all, making it very easy to keep their coats clean and shiny. If there is one downside to this, it is that because they don't require much hands-on attention, often they get less nail and ear care, making it even more important to start handling their paws and ears at a very young age to get them used to being touched and handled. A dog with a low-maintenance coat could very quickly turn into a high-maintenance dog if every time we want to check his ears and nails we need to assemble a small army of people to get near him with nail clippers or a cotton ball.

Grooming Frequency

I have a simple rule of thumb when it comes to how frequently one should groom a dog. When the dog is no longer huggable, it is time to give him a bath. The dog's living environment will also help determine how often you have to bathe him. A dog that lives in a New York City apartment will get dirty very quickly just by walking around the block, especially if it's raining. A dog that lives in a house with a well-manicured lawn will keep himself clean much longer, and by rolling in the fresh grass, he will give himself a "spa" treatment that we pay lots of money for in the big city.

The pet industry has a wide variety of shampoos for frequent baths that will clean the dog without removing the coat's natural oils. As a general rule, the more frequently you plan to bathe your dog, the milder the shampoo should be. Whitening and clarifying shampoos are usually the strongest shampoos because they are designed to strip the buildup of products that you have already used on your dog, and they will allow the light to reflect more and give the coat a more "glowing" illusion or appearance. Puppy and hypoallergenic shampoos are usually the mildest.

Hair Type

Short Hair

Most short-haired dogs have a straight layer of coat that lies flat against the skin. They can be divided into two categories.

Short Hair with Single Coat

Examples of breeds with this coat are Italian greyhounds, Weimaraners, and Doberman pinschers.

Their bodies are covered with a very fine layer of shiny hair very tight to the skin. This kind of coat is very low maintenance. It is important to protect these dogs from extreme heat and cold because their coat doesn't provide the insulation that dogs with double coats have. Sweaters and jackets are not just a fashion accessory—they are a must in extreme weather conditions.

Single short-haired dogs don't shed and don't need to be bathed as often. Going over the coat with a damp washcloth and a little self-rinse shampoo or just warm water is enough to bring the shine back to the coat after a day at the park.

This coat doesn't need much attention, but a good rub down with a rubber brush will feel great and keep the blood circulation at full speed to keep the coat healthy and super shiny.

Short Hair with Double Coat

Examples of breeds with this coat are pugs, Chihuahuas, and dalmatians.

Their coat is tight to the skin but feels thicker and cushiony to the touch. The thin layer of undercoat is not always visible on these dogs, but it surely makes an appearance when the dog has been lying on the sofa for a while and leaves a nest-shaped layer of dead coat on it. Dogs with this kind of coat need more attention than single-coated dogs because they constantly shed dead hairs. Using the right brushes will help to strengthen the hair follicles, significantly reducing the amount of shedding. Even though this dog's coat won't get matted, it will get smelly if not washed every couple of weeks, depending on where your dog lives, plays, and so on.

We might look low-maintenance but our short, dense coats will shed a lot.

Medium Hair

Most dogs with medium-hair length have a double coat. These dogs can be divided into wiry or straight coats.

Most terriers have medium-length coats with a wiry texture. These dogs get "hand-stripped." Maintaining the coat with a regular hand-stripping technique will keep its texture and color. Using clippers on a dog with a wiry coat will most likely change the coat to a softer texture, making it lose some of its bright colors and requiring more frequent grooming.

Examples of breeds with this coat are cairn terriers, fox terriers, and West Highland white terriers (Westies).

We might not have soft, flowing hair but our wiry coats, when groomed properly, will rarely smell.

Dogs with medium double straight coats present a straight outer coat and a soft woolly layer of fine undercoat.

This kind of coat needs to be brushed often to prevent the undercoat from getting packed, which will create mats and expose the dog to sores and hot spots. While brushing this kind of coat, it is important to use the right tools to ensure that you are reaching the undercoat. It is not unusual to meet a dog owner who swears that his or her dog gets daily brushing but still gets matted. If this is the case, then most likely the brushing was done only on the top layer, letting the undercoat get packed and matted. An undercoat rake is a great tool to use on these kinds of dogs.

Examples of breeds with this coat are German shepherds, Shiba Innus, Siberian huskies, and Labrador retrievers, just to name a few. Keeping the undercoat properly brushed will help the dog to adjust to extreme weather conditions, because the undercoat creates an insulating layer that protects the dog from heat and cold.

Our undercoats are our wardrobes and we like to change them every season. The only way to avoid hair bunnies taking over the house is by brushing us with the proper tools and techniques.

Long Hair

Most breeds with long coats can be divided into drop or straight coats and curly coats, with or without undercoat. Long-haired dogs need a very strict grooming schedule to prevent matting.

Long Drop Coat with Undercoat

Examples of breeds with this coat are shih tzus, Tibetan terriers, and bearded collies.

This kind of coat is long and flows elegantly when the dog moves, and the undercoat is soft and woolly.

Don't hate us because we are beautiful. Keeping up these looks takes a lot of work!

Long Fluffy Coat with Undercoat

Examples of breeds with this coat are Pomeranians, Pekingese, and Old English sheepdogs.

These dogs present long coats with an intense presence of undercoat. Their outer coats are straight with a coarse texture that makes them stand up with a fabulous mane effect, giving the name to a popular style, the lion cut.

Clipping this kind of coat short can alter the pattern of how the hair will grow back.

Dogs with long fluffy coats are fairly high maintenance because they can get matted quickly if not brushed often.

Long Drop Coat without Undercoat

Examples of breeds with this coat are Yorkshire terriers, Maltese, and Afghan hounds.

This kind of hair, when kept healthy, is easier to care for than hair with an undercoat. This hair is very similar to human hair, soft and long. Dogs with this kind of coat do renew their hair, but their shedding is minimum and not seasonal. A good weekly brushing will keep the coat nice and shiny. Using thinning shears when trimming will produce natural-looking results.

Long and flowing coats equals a lot of time spent brushing.

Images courtesy of Shutterstock.com

A beautiful, fluffy hairdo can easily turn into a bad case of pillow head if not brushed often enough.

Poodle image courtesy of Shutterstock.com

Long Curly Hair

Examples of breeds with this coat are poodles, bichons frises, and Portuguese water dogs.

Most curly coats don't have an undercoat, and this is the reason they are the most hypoallergenic kind. However, no dog is totally hypoallergenic because saliva contains proteins that can trigger some human allergies.

These are the perfect dogs for fabulous scissor work. It is necessary to keep the curls brushed properly to avoid matting. The use of snap-on comb attachments makes it easy to keep them at a medium-length coat.

TIP

Shaving Warning

Although some pet owners feel that clipping down double-coated dogs is a necessary solution to excessive shedding and seasonal problems, the hair on some double-coated dogs will grow back very patchy after being shaved.

Out of all the theories on this issue, I believe that when a double-coated dog is clipped down short, because the outer coat and undercoat come from the same hair follicle, the undercoat will curl before it comes out and block the follicle, not allowing the new healthy coat to come out.

Gently using a de-shedding blade on the dog after he has been clipped down has shown very good results when combined with a weekly bath using a bristle brush to open up the hair follicles.

An important thing to keep in mind and avoid is that if the dog has underlying health conditions, such as a hormonal imbalance or a thyroid problem, these issues can be brought to the surface by shaving his coats. Shaving not only can make them visible, but sometimes these health conditions also will be reflected in the newly grown coat.

The use of an attachment comb on a double-coated dog could solve this problem, but it will require the dog to be very clean and perfectly combed out to allow the attachment comb to run through the coat.

Using a #10 blade on the clippers with the attachment comb will make it easier.

Anatomy Chart

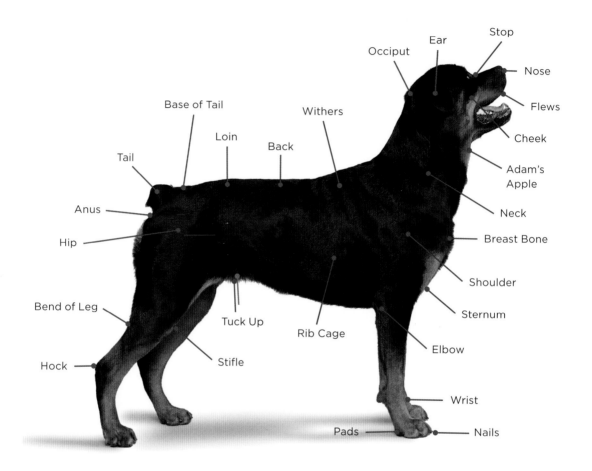

Occiput

Ear

Stop

Nose

Flews

Cheek

Adam's Apple

Neck

Breast Bone

Shoulder

Sternum

Elbow

Wrist

Nails

Pads

Base of Tail

Withers

Loin

Back

Tail

Anus

Hip

Bend of Leg

Tuck Up

Rib Cage

Stifle

Hock

Nails

Unattended nails are a common but avoidable problem. Not only do they look bad and make it more difficult to properly trim, but they also present a serious health hazard for your dog. Excessively long nails make it difficult for a dog to walk properly and stand up correctly and, if left unattended, will quickly lead to serious back problems.

How often you trim a dog's nails will depend on the lifestyle of your pet. Active dogs wear out nails while running and consequently will require fewer nail trims. Pampered indoor pooches need more attention. A good rule of thumb, or paw, is to clip nails every three to four weeks.

Anatomy of the Nail

The very tip of the nail, also known as the hollow part of the nail (or nail shell), is the safest and, in my opinion, only place for a home groomer to cut. For white nails, the tip can be identified by holding the nail up to the light to see the whitest part of the nail. Darker nails require a closer look. You can identify the cuttable tip of a dark nail by looking at the nail from the bottom and finding the hollow and veinless tip. Beyond the tip of the nail is the main body of the nail that also contains the vein, commonly called the quick.

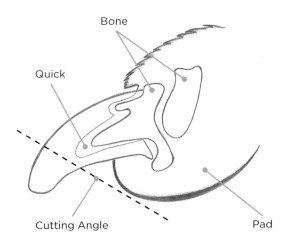

Bone

Quick

Cutting Angle

Pad

Ears

Describing the location of a dog's ears is pretty easy and standard: They are located at each side of the dog's head. But with so many recognized breeds, describing every type of ear shape takes a little longer.

Understanding the dog's ears is important because their shape will give us an indication of how much care they will need. For example, usually ears with free airflow around them are naturally kept dry and clean, making them less susceptible to ear infections.

Regardless of the shape of the ear, they all share a similar anatomy of the ear canal. It is important to know how the ear is constructed to understand the importance of proper care.

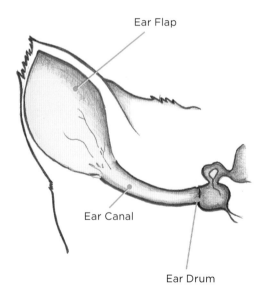

Ear Flap

Ear Canal

Ear Drum

Often, how much grooming attention ears need depends on their shape. Ears that allow a free flow of air are usually the ones that will do just fine with a weekly wipe.

Ear shapes that cover the ear canal need more attention because they have a tendency to develop ear infections due to the humidity that can easily accumulate inside the ear canal—a bacteria-friendly environment. It is necessary to check and clean these types of ears at least once a week. The complete ear cleaning process is described in chapter 4.

Examples of some of the most common ears and their shapes are as follows:

Button-shaped ears can be found on the Jack Russell and the pug.

Rose-shaped ears are found on the skinny whippet and the bulky bulldog.

The collie and the Airedale terrier share semipricked ears.

Pricked ears are triangular in shape, proportional to the head size, and point up like those of the Alaskan malamute and the Australian cattle dog.

Drop ears with or without folds lie flat on each side of the dog's head. Ears without folds are like those of the basset hound or folded like those of the vizsla.

Bat ears are larger in size—almost too large for the head—and point slightly to the sides, like those of the corgi and the Chihuahua.

Left: Blunt ears are similar in shape to bat ears but, as indicated by the name, have rounded tips. A perfect example of this type of ear is found on the French bulldog.

Right: Cropped ears are the ones that have been surgically modified, like on the Great Dane, Doberman pinscher, or schnauzers.

Paws

Dogs come built with their own all-terrain shoes: their paws. Their paw pads are like cushions and reduce the impact on the bones, have a texture that keeps dogs from slipping, and protect them against extreme temperatures.

Mother Nature didn't plan for our dogs to live in congested cities, walking on egg-frying hot pavement and all the chemicals and garbage that they encounter during even just a short walk around the block. It is important to periodically inspect your dog's paws to be sure that they are healthy and clean.

Because most dogs only sweat through their tongues and their pads, when hair gets matted in between their toes, the humidity released by sweating will turn their paws into the perfect environment for the growth of bacteria. Bacteria are one of the main reasons for hair discoloration.

The use of a pet paw balm on the pads will create an insulating layer that will protect your dog's paws from extreme temperatures and even chemicals.

If your dog enjoys digging at the dog park, be sure to remove dirt and debris accumulated at the base of and in between his nails and toes.

It is important to wipe your dog's paws after each walk in the city. Chemicals used to clean sidewalks and ice-melting products sometimes have a sweet taste that can turn your dog's paws into a toxic treat. If your dog is licking his paws; make sure they are clean.

Like our own feet, dog's paws have many nerve endings. For this reason, they will enjoy a paw massage as much as we enjoy a foot massage. Not only will they find it relaxing, but it is also a great way to get dogs accustomed to having their paws touched, which will make nail trimming and grooming much easier.

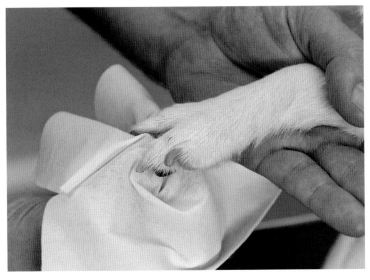

The nonslippery texture of the paw's pads can easily pick up debris, gum, and all sorts funky stuff that you probably don't want on your sofa.

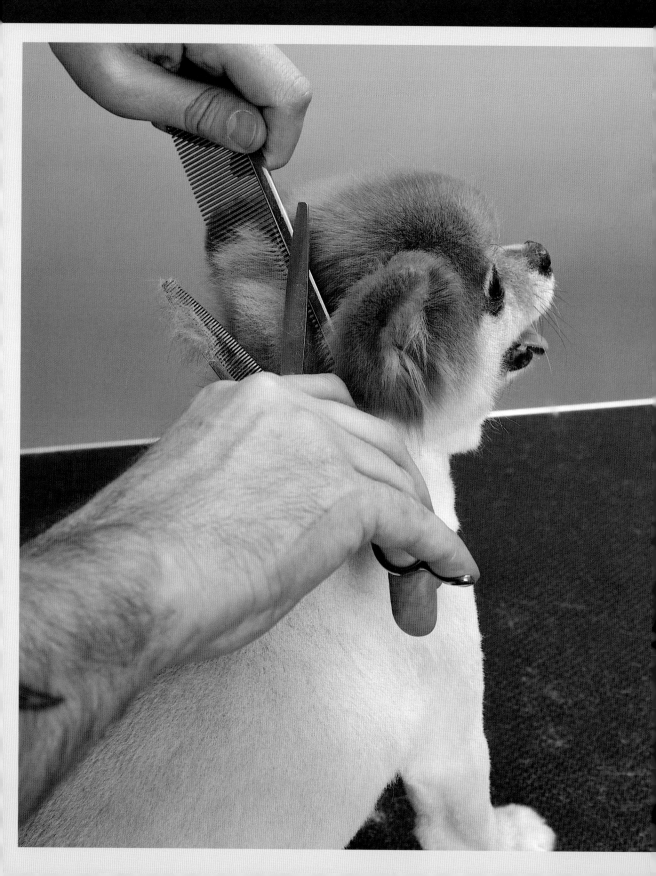

CHAPTER 2

Tools

Although shopping for grooming tools can bring you to an exciting new territory filled with funny-looking, bright-colored tools, choosing the right equipment to work on your own dog will require you to have a clear idea of what kind of coat you are going to be working on and why.

Decide whether you are planning to just "touch up" the work of a professional groomer to extend the visits to the salon a couple of extra weeks by neatening the face, privates, and paws; give your dog a "smooth" (very short clip down) to get through the summer without having to spend much time shaking sand or twigs out of his coat; or go full creative and really take charge of your dog grooming needs and style. These are some of the things to consider when choosing tools to get the job done.

I once showed up at a client's house having forgotten my "perfect" professional tools and had to do a grooming with a pair of kitchen scissors. This humbling experience helped remind me of the importance of having the proper tools handy.

Brushes

With so many brushes on the market, one can easily get the impression that you have to purchase many different brushes to do a proper grooming, when in fact, the key is to choose the right brush for each purpose. Specific brushes are used before, during, and after the bath. It is a good idea to have one brush to use when the dog is dirty and matted and a second brush to use when the dog is clean.

I recommend using less expensive brushes for prep work (before bathing) and a better brush or set of brushes for working on clean hair. This will not only extend your "finishing" tools' life span, but also save you time from having to disinfect and wash the brushes you used to brush out mud when it is time to get busy on the grooming task. You can clean and disinfect later. Your dog will appreciate these time-saving techniques and, more importantly, being able to complete the grooming more quickly will be safer for your dog because he will spend less time on the grooming table or surface.

Slicker Brush

The slicker brush is the one-size-fits-all brush. Slicker brushes are usually rectangular. They have a solid base with a soft rubber insert that holds many metal bristles. This soft rubber insert allows all the bristles to bend in the same direction.

The shorter the bristles, the more undercoat they will pull out because there will be more pull and less give of the hair follicles. For longer coats, a slicker brush with a softer back and longer bristles will have more "give" and flexibility, making it easier to go through a thicker or longer coat.

Slicker brushes should only be used when the coat is dry, before bathing and after bathing when the hair has been towel dried and you are brushing the dog while using the hair dryer. Using the slicker brush on wet hair could scratch the skin.

Dog hair is elastic when damp, so you have to be especially careful when using any tools on your dog while the hair is wet.

Using a Slicker Brush

The proper way to hold a slicker brush is to pinch the brush handle using your thumb and middle finger. Placing your index finger on the top portion of the handle, where the brush weight is evenly distributed, allows you to regulate the pressure you apply to the different parts of the body. Gripping the brush too tightly will cause you to lose sensitivity and control of the brush. Maintain brush control with careful wrist movements and index finger pressure. **(1, 2**, and **3)**

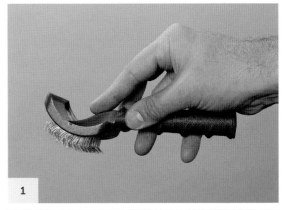

The best way to achieve a great result is to brush your dog section by section, making sure the section you are working on is totally brushed and dry before moving to the next section. The width of each section should be the same as the width of your brush or comb.

For maximum fluff, always stroke with the brush under the warm air of a dryer.

Using the slicker brush before the bath will help to separate the hair, making it easy for the shampoo to penetrate all the way down to the skin where it will most effectively clean the skin and coat.

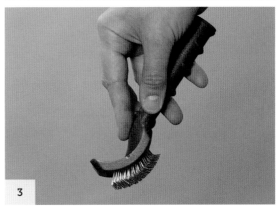

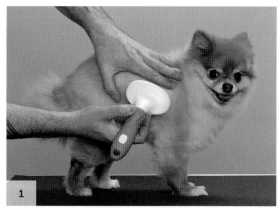

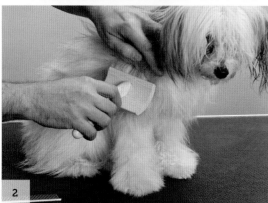

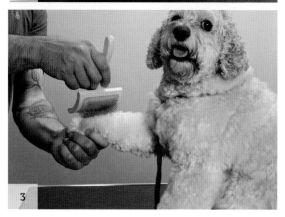

On areas where the skin is loose, it is recommended to use your free hand to softly stretch the skin, running the brush line by line; this process is called line-brushing. **(1)**

On long-haired dogs, a slicker brush will help to remove mats, will loosen dead undercoat, and will remove dead skin cells while promoting strong and healthy skin circulation and strengthening the hair follicles.

On drop-coat breeds (Yorkie, Maltese, and bearded collie), brushing in the direction of the hair growth will leave the hair slick, flat, and shiny. **(2)**

On curly or fluffy coats (poodle, chow chow, and Pomeranian), brushing against the hair growth will emphasize the dog's natural volume. **(3)**

On dogs with medium-length hair, a slicker brush will remove the dead undercoat, reinforce the skin's blood circulation, and strengthen the hair follicles to reduce shedding. When used after the bath, a slicker brush will give the coat a shiny finish.

Pin Brush

Pin brushes come in many shapes and sizes with a wide range of pin lengths and pin flexibilities. They perform the best on coats in good condition that are already free of mats. The softer the base of the pin brush, the more flexible the brush will be.

Dogs with heavier or thicker undercoat will benefit from firmer brushes to make sure every hair is lifted and fluffed to perfection. On dogs with a drop coat, using a pin brush will result in a perfectly smooth look.

Bristle Brush

Although this brush is not commonly used, it is a good tool to give short-haired dogs a shiny finish and to remove dandruff and loose hair. It is a good training brush because dogs feel like they are getting a massage when this brush is used.

Rubber Curry Brush

This brush will probably be your dog's favorite because he will feel like he is getting a finger massage. This tool is perfect to use in the tub while bathing dogs with short and medium coats. This brush is also useful for short-haired dogs that shed. It easily lifts and removes dead hair, and the dogs love their massage.

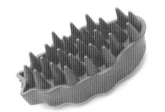

Face and Paw Brushes

There is nothing better than a good soft brush to deeply clean your dog. It is important to remember that dirt and debris get caught on paws, under the nails, and in the thin skin between the pads. A natural, soft nailbrush or even a veggie brush is useful to be sure our friend's paws get perfectly clean. I love to use a good brush on the body of short- and medium-haired dogs to really get the skin clean and remove dead skin cells. A small enough brush will even help remove tearstains and mouth stains.

Image courtesy of Shutterstock.com

Rake

A rake is a tool with a handle and a wide head containing one or more rows of rigid, rounded teeth (usually widely spaced) designed to remove dead undercoat on dogs with medium- to long-length hair and a thick undercoat. Select a rake whose pins are approximately the same length as the dog's coat to be sure it penetrates enough to open and remove the undercoat but not long enough to risk scratching your dog's skin.

Use small strokes at the beginning while holding the dog's skin taut. As the undercoat starts to loosen, make longer strokes with the undercoat rake, always being aware of how deep you are going to avoid scratching the dog's skin. After the undercoat feels loose, use a slicker brush to remove the loose coat.

Mat-Breaking Rake

This small tool with a handle and one or more rows of sharp-bladed teeth, when used properly and with extreme caution, is a great tool to help break severe mats. Using small strokes, apply directly on mats to open or loosen them before using a slicker brush. It must be used very carefully because the blades are sharp and can easily cut your dog's ears, tail, or loose skin. Always hold the mat with your fingers next to the skin to avoid unnecessary pulling and to protect the skin. Start by opening the mat from the outer edge, moving slowly into the middle of the mat. Avoid using mat-breaking rakes on the ear flaps and on the tail because these can easily get in contact with the blades.

De-shedding Blade

This is a tool with a handle and a serrated blade at the end. These blades are good to remove the top layer of dead coat on medium-haired breeds such as German shepherds or golden retrievers. By running it on top of the coat, always following the direction the coat grows, the teeth will grab and pull the undercoat. This tool should be used very carefully to avoid hurting the dog's skin, especially while raking the edges and sensitive areas of the dog.

Stripping Knife

The stripping knife is a grooming tool with a handle and a small metal finely serrated blade specifically designed for dogs that need to be hand-stripped. Hand-stripping is a grooming technique that pulls the dead hair from dogs with wiry coats, usually terriers. When used properly, with the correct hand motion and application of pressure, it will remove the dead coat and excess undercoat. The hair must be pulled in the direction of the hair growth.

While holding the skin taut with one hand, grab a few hairs between the blade and the thumb of your other hand. Keeping your wrist straight, move the arm that's pulling the hair out and away from the skin. Rolling or twisting your wrist will make this technique uncomfortable for the dog. You also can perform this technique without the stripping knife, by just using your fingers to neaten the appearance of the dog.

A stripping knife can be used to finish sporting-style haircuts by running the stripping blade from head to tail along the dog's back to erase clipper marks and give a natural finished look.

Combs

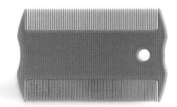

Flea Combs

This is the best tool to use when searching for fleas and ticks. For the novice groomer, plastic flea combs are the best because of their flexibility. They are also the safest ones to use when working around the face to remove any dry discharge around the eyes. Before using these combs to remove goop around the eyes, first soak the area in diluted tearless shampoo, being careful not to allow shampoo to drip into the eyes. Flea combs should only be run through a previously de-matted coat.

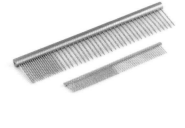

Steel Combs

Stainless steel–toothed combs are the best, most durable, and easiest to clean and disinfect. They come in a wide selection of shapes and even colors. Fine- and medium-tooth steel combs are about 7½ inches (19.1 cm) long and are versatile enough for use on most breeds. Combs that have smaller and tighter tooth separation are better suited for faces and topknots. Combs with wider tooth separation are best suited for the body.

Rat-Tail Combs

Rat-tail combs are especially good to finish up faces and make the perfect ponytail.

Be sure to choose one with rounded teeth to avoid any possibility of hurting your dog. The metal tail part of the comb can be used to slowly open up mats.

Shears

Let's talk about the difference between scissors and shears.

Scissors are usually small, with both handles approximately the same size. This tool is most commonly used for small cutting projects.

Shears, on the other hand, are designed to better fit the anatomy of the hand, providing more stability for a clean and controlled cut. The handles are of different lengths with more room to rest the fingers. Most shears come with a knob to control the pressure between the blades.

Dog grooming shears should only be used to cut hair. It is a good idea to have more than one pair of shears: one to be used during prep work, to remove mats that cannot be brushed out or just to remove unnecessary hair before the bath, and a second, better pair of shears, to execute and finish your grooming job.

Shears are a groomer's most delicate tools. Keeping them sharp and clean will make your job easier with better results. Maintenance of your shears is very important. Never cut ribbons or paper with your grooming shears. Grooming scissors and shears should be used for grooming only.

Shears can be divided into three categories, which we'll discuss in the following section.

Straight shears, with a variety of options in size, weigh, and length, can be used on a variety of coat types.

Thinning shears have both a straight and tooth-edged blade and are useful in removing bulk. They are also used in trimming and finishing techniques.

Curved shears might take some practice getting used to, but are helpful in achieving nice round edges in your grooming.

Straight Shears

Straight shears come in a wide variety of shapes, lengths, and weights. Shears with a thicker blade are good for heavier coats, like on cocker spaniels or Portuguese water dogs. Shears with thinner blades are better for trimming and sculpting dogs with curly hair and no undercoat, like on bichons frises or poodles.

Thinning Shears

Thinning shears are used to blend different areas of the coat—and they are your best friend when it comes to disguising minor mistakes. One of its two blades is straight and regular while the other blade has teeth. Whether the thinning shears will blend more—or less—will depend on the number of teeth it has.

Thinning shears are great for thinning out bulky hair. They can be used on tails, around feet, and around skirts. They not only reduce the length of the coat but the amount or density of hair around areas such as the neck and hips, giving the dog a more elegant appearance and a neater outline. They are perfect for breeds such as golden retrievers or other dogs that require an all-around trim to maintain a natural look.

I always finish my work by going over the dog with thinning shears to soften up the edges.

Curved Shears

Curved shears come in many different lengths and curved angles and are great to finish round heads and trim around the feet. The more you use curved shears, the more you are going to like them. Curved shears sized 7½ inches (19.1 cm) are versatile enough to handle most pet grooming tasks. For small dogs, you will need smaller curved shears, especially for trimming around their ears.

Choosing the Right Shears

This is a good place to mention again that all your grooming tools should feel comfortable and balanced in your hands. You will work with more confidence when your shears feel as if they are an extension of your hands. The best way to choose a good pair of shears or scissors is to place the pair in your hand, balancing it in your palm to be sure its weight is evenly distributed between the blades and the handles.

Most major shear companies carry both top-of-the-line shears and a more affordable line. Generally, they all follow the same design lines, so your best bet is to get less-expensive shears from a good company rather than a tool from a company that only offers cheaper or low-quality products.

Reputable, well-established companies will try to gain your trust and your business, hoping that you will eventually upgrade your equipment with them.

Caring for Your Shears

It is important to take good care of all your sharp grooming tools. Keeping them clean, well maintained, and in good working order will help ensure a good result. Using the oil that the manufacturer recommends is the safest way to keep them sharp and free of rust. Be aware that dropping your shears on a hard surface can ruin them. Working over a soft mat will help avoid costly accidents.

When choosing a pair of shears, I test for a balanced feel by resting them in my palm. A good pair of shears will help you to be more comfortable and confident in your grooming.

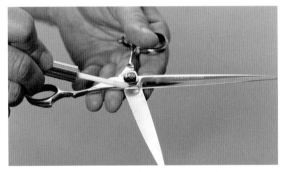

Shears should be sharp, free of rust, and move smoothly.

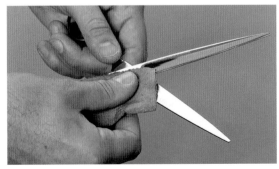

Proper care of your shears includes rubbing them with the manufacturer recommended oil and handling with care.

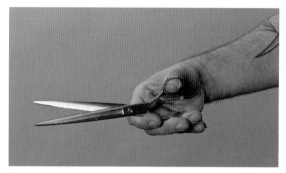

Keep a straight wrist and use only your thumb to open and close the shears, which means one blade will stay stationary while the other moves up and down.

Practice makes perfect. Once you feel comfortable, add movement of your forearm to direct the blade.

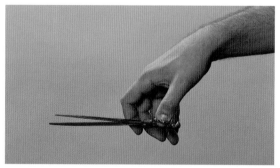

Notice how my wrist and hand have remained in the same position, while my hand has turned to change the angle of my shears.

Using Your Shears

Giving yourself time to get acquainted with the shears' weight and balance is essential to working with more confidence and having better control, leading to a much better result.

Once you have selected shears that fit comfortably in your hand, it is time to train your hand on how to make them work properly.

Doing some exercises and getting your muscles accustomed to the shears and how to use them correctly will take some time, but soon using them will become second nature. Eventually your focus will be on what you are cutting, not how you are cutting.

Start by holding the shears keeping a straight wrist. Next, try opening them moving only your thumb while the rest of your hand stays still. Your thumb should always be resting and relaxed through the hole to give your hand a bigger range of motion.

Continue practicing opening and closing until you feel that you can effortlessly operate the shears by moving only your thumb. After you feel comfortable, add the movement of your forearm, using your forearm to direct the shears in different directions. (I did say your forearm, not your wrist.) Keeping control of the direction of the shears with your forearm will give you better control, producing a much cleaner cut. Moving your wrist will change the angle of the blades, resulting in an uneven cut.

At first, using shears feels unnatural, like you are doing a "robot dance," but eventually your body will become so familiar with the movement that you almost won't even notice you are doing it.

Clippers

It is important to choose the clippers that will work best for your dog. The pet industry offers a large selection of clippers, from very light and inexpensive trimmers good for whiskers and ears **(1)** to more heavy-duty clippers with adjustable or interchangeable blades for different lengths of hair. **(2)**

Most clipper companies share the same blade model numbers to identify the length of hair left on the dog. Clippers made for human hair have their own numerical identification system. Referring to the blade chart (page 44) will allow you to compare blades according to their size in millimeters.

Clippers come in corded or cordless models. Most professionals use corded clippers, which tend to be more durable, have more power, and will not lose power as the battery starts to run out. As with all your cutting tools, proper maintenance of your clippers will make your job easier.

How to Hold

It is important to hold clippers at an angle, with the base of the blade parallel to the skin, and move them with an even and steady speed for a smooth finish. If you move clippers too quickly, the blades won't be able to cut the hair and will pull on it instead.

Hold clippers with a firm but gentle touch. Holding the clippers too tightly will reduce your hand's sensitivity and its ability to follow the dog's body shape. The clippers should rest comfortably in your hand. Keeping the blade parallel with the skin will enable you to apply gentle pressure without scratching or pinching your dog. Avoid "scooping" with the clippers; remember that the tip of the blade is sharp. Practice makes perfect; the more you use clippers, the more they will become an extension of your hand.

1

The pet market offers a wide range of clippers; choosing the right kind will help you achieve great results.

2

This type of clipper allows you to switch out blades to adjust the length of the haircut. A power cord lets you take the time you need without worrying about battery life.

Handling the clippers with a firm but gentle touch will allow you to feel and follow your dog's body shape.

For Matted Hair

If you are shaving down a dog with matted hair, it is crucial to keep the skin taut and constantly look at the blade to avoid it pulling on the hair by bringing the skin too close to the blade. If the dog is severely matted, use a pair of round-tip scissors to carefully open up an area to start clipping by cutting a line through the mat. Never use the scissors with the blades perpendicular to the skin. Pulling a mat away from the body will also pull the skin up with it and dangerously close to the scissor blades. When cutting mats, keep the scissors parallel to the skin, moving only the blade that you can see.

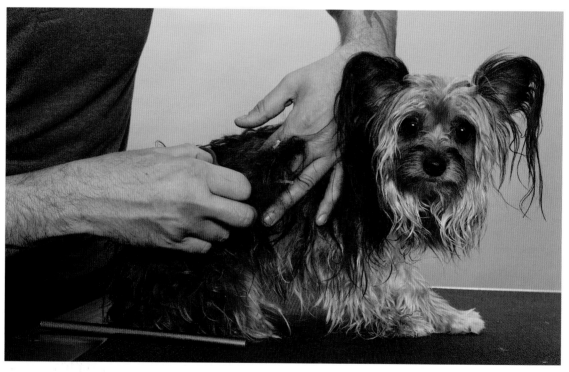

Preventing matting takes dedication; removing mats takes patience. Working slowly will keep your dog relaxed and let you work on your makeover project.

How to Use

To get a feel for the clippers, situate yourself behind the dog and begin clipping from the back of the dog's neck down to the tail, with the blade facing you. Unless a specific cut indicates differently, you should always clip dog hair in the direction that it grows, from the back of the neck to the tail and from the top to the bottom on the sides and legs. **(1)**

Always be very careful when approaching places where the skin is loose as blades can pinch loose skin and injure your dog. Keeping the skin taut using your free hand is a good way to help you move the clippers along smoothly. **(2)**

After a few minutes of constant use, the clipper blades will get hot. Therefore, it is important to constantly check the blade temperature on your forearm to avoid irritating or burning your dog's skin. When you feel that the blade is getting hot, stop immediately and use a blade cooling spray or let the blades rest on a cold surface for a few minutes. While waiting for the blades to cool, you can use this time to go over other parts of grooming such as checking the nails, using scissors around the head, or just giving your dog a break and a quick massage to reassure him that everything is okay.

In order for the clippers to leave a smooth finish, while using the longer blades, the coat should be clean and properly brushed out to avoid uneven patches.

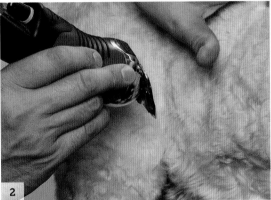

Begin simply by standing behind your dog and clipping from neck to tail with the clippers pointed towards you. Remember not to hold the clipper too tightly so you have the right sensitivity and control.

Attachments

Most clipper companies offer a variety of attachment combs that, when secured over the blade, will allow you different hair length options. These attachments are great when you want a longer hair length and will save on time spent using scissors. For best results when using attachment combs, the hair should be perfectly brushed and free of mats. Attachment combs should only be used with a #30 blade unless another blade is recommended.

Caring for Your Clipper and Blade

Clippers and blades, like any other cutting blade, should be cleaned after each use with products recommended by the manufacturer. Leaving hair on blades could result in oxidation that will make your blades dull.

This chart gives you an idea of the different blade sizes.

BLADE NUMBER	LENGTH OF HAIR	BODY	STOMACH	FACE	EARS	PADS	RECTUM	MATTED
#30	1/50" (0.5 mm)					●		
#10	1/16" (1.6 mm)		●	●	●		●	
#8½	7/64" (2.8 mm)		●	●				●
#7F	1/8" (3.2 mm)							●
#5F	1/4" (6.4 mm)	●						●
#4F	3/8" (9.5 mm)	●						
#3¾	1/2" (12.7 mm)	●						

Nail Care

Everybody will notice if a dog is matted or dirty, but because a dog's nails are less visible, they can easily be overlooked. I can't tell you how many times I have even heard pet owners tell me that they prefer long nails because they "look cute." Another, more understandable, reason for unkept nails is fear. Many people are terrified by the idea of clipping their dog's nails. Regardless of the reason, long nails can present serious health problems for dogs.

Unkempt nails will alter the natural position of the foot, shifting the toe bones and affecting the whole alignment of the leg, which in turn can cause long-term back problems. Picture yourself walking in uncomfortable shoes for a very long time and the effect that would have on the way you walk.

Generally speaking, the size of your dog and his nails will determine the size of nail trimmer to use. Additionally, for every size of nail there is more than one style or model of clippers to choose from. To narrow your search, after you have determined the size you need, it is important to consider what style best fits your hand and which will be better for your dog's disposition.

Whatever style you choose, you should always have some styptic powder on hand. Styptic powder contains an antihemorrhagic component that contracts tissue and seals injured blood vessels within seconds. A bleeding nail is not a medical emergency but can be scary and messy if you don't have the proper product to stop the bleeding. If you find yourself in this unfortunate situation, pack cornstarch on the tip of the nail and hold it for a couple of minutes.

Guillotine nail clippers really do resemble the full size version; a blade moves across the hole to clip the nail tip.

Scissor-shaped nail clippers are comfortable and easy to use for smaller dogs.

Guillotine Nail Clippers

Guillotine nail clippers have an opening into which you place the dog's nail. When you squeeze the handle, a single sharp blade closes the opening and clips the nail.

Pros: The design of the clippers makes it easy to find the right angle to cut because the blades are at the same level as the bottom part. The design also makes it easy to go through thick nails without much effort.

Cons: The clippers come in different sizes, but because the nail has to go through a hole, in my opinion, it makes it harder to have good visibility —a task made even more difficult when the dog has long hair or small paws.

Scissor-Shaped Nail Clippers

Scissor-shaped nail clippers look like a small pair of regular scissors with a semicircle-shaped opening on the blade where the nail rests.

Pros: They are very comfortable to handle because they function just like a regular pair of scissors. They most commonly come in a small size and are very safe to use on small claws without much hassle. They are perfect for small breeds and don't look scary, which in turn will keep you more calm.

Cons: They aren't the best option for large dogs or dogs with very strong nails.

Pliers-Shaped Trimmers

This type of trimmer is my personal favorite because it is easy to use, it comes in different sizes, and most of them have a safety stop to avoid cutting the nail too short.

Electric Grinders

Electric grinders are great for dogs that have been trained since a young age to tolerate their paws being handled a lot. The dog will tolerate the vibration of the grinder against the nail only if he feels your confidence and trusts you. Electric grinders are a great finishing tool to smooth the edges of the nails, especially in dogs with skin problems that scratch themselves often and if the nail has grown too long and needs to be shortened a bit. Once the nail is short, the regular use of the grinder will cut a great deal of the time needed to maintain the nail length.

Nail Files

Nail files for dogs are similar to the human counterpart and are usually built of a much stronger material with a more comfortable handle.

Any nail clipping method will leave the edges of the nails very sharp, making it dangerous not only to a new pair of stockings but could turn a happy welcome dance into a scratching match. Filing the nails after they have been clipped will round off the edges, making it safer for both dogs and humans.

Pros: They are good to smooth out the edges after clipping.

Cons: If the dog doesn't like to get his nails trimmed and filing is the only alternative, it will take a long time to file a long nail to the desired length.

My favorite style nail clipper is the plier-shaped trimmer because of the size options and safety features.

A nail file can be just the trick to avoid being scratched by newly trimmed nails.

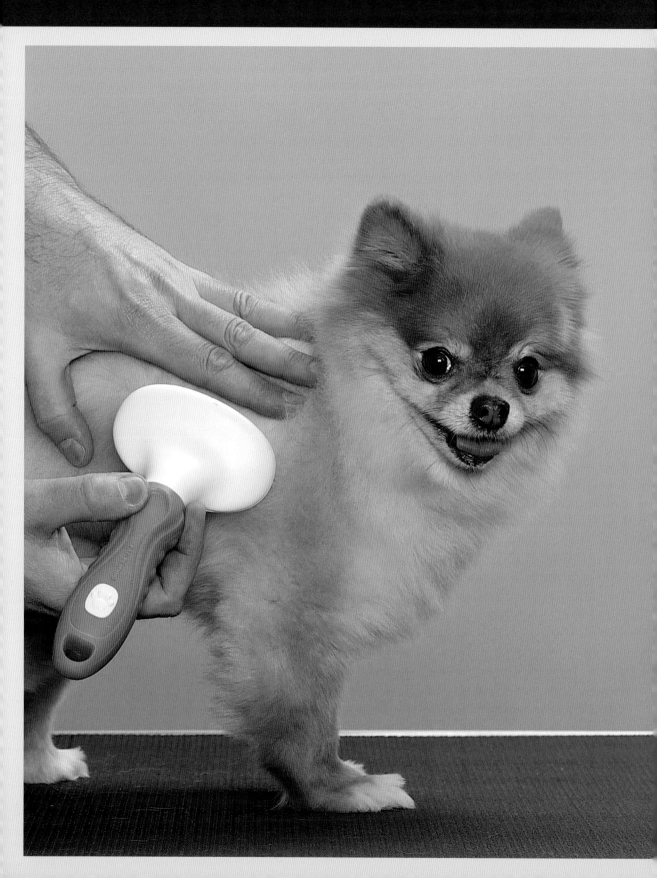

CHAPTER 3

Brushing

Brushing a dog plays not only an important role in keeping him in good shape but also is the most important tool for early detection of many health issues.

Brushing your dog correctly will provide visual contact with every inch of the dog's body, making it easier to identify scratches, bumps, allergic skin irritations, ear problems, fleas and other parasites, and the list goes on. Some problems that are discovered early enough can be treated at home. Those that require veterinary care will probably come with more manageable vet bills because they were discovered early, but, most important, early detection will most likely be less painful for the dog and provide a greater chance of a faster healing. When overlooked, minor issues can escalate and become expensive, painful, and sometimes life-threatening health problems.

On an emotional level, brushing is very similar to petting. In the wild, grooming is one of the actions that will establish social status and one of the main bonding experiences. By brushing your dog, you are establishing who is in charge, and you will send a message of love, caring, and protection, making the relationship with your dog much deeper and gaining the dog's respect and trust.

Daily Brushing

Regardless of the kind of coat the dog has, daily brushing will prevent long coats from matting, remove dead coat, and reinforce the blood circulation to the top layers of the skin, tightening up the hair follicles. This keeps the coat and skin in great shape, reduces shedding and ingrown hairs (which can trigger hot spots), and helps to distribute the dog's natural oils, keeping the hair healthy and shiny.

Handling Mats

The best way to handle mats is to prevent them from happening in the first place. Dog hair gets matted not only from lack of care but also from everyday situations, making it difficult to keep long coats from matting.

Dogs with allergies can easily develop skin issues that cause the body to produce an excessive amount of oil, irritating the skin to a point at which the dog will be very uncomfortable while being brushed. The use of certain medications or anesthesia can cause hair loss or sudden shedding that will turn a healthy coat into a mess in just a couple of days. Female dogs usually lose a good amount of coat after they go into heat or after having puppies.

Although these realities can relieve you of some of the guilt, it is still important to react as soon as possible to avoid the matting problem from getting worse and escalating to bigger health issues. If you are determined to save as much of a matted dog coat as possible, it is important to take into consideration the total time that it will take to de-mat the coat. Often it's best to divide the total time into short sessions, sometimes over a few days, to prevent aggravating or hurting your dog.

I decided to wear dreadlocks for a while (dreadlocks are just well-manicured matts). When I was over that fad, I tried to de-mat myself. At that point I realized firsthand how dogs must feel—and yes, I used dog grooming de-matting tools. Since then, I've become very aware of how dogs feel and I do my best to keep them from getting matted. Choosing a practical short hairstyle can also keep the dog from an unnecessary, uncomfortable, and sometimes painful experience that could trigger a long-lasting fear of being groomed.

De-matting

Before you get to the de-matting process, it is important to prepare the coat as much as possible to make the job easier for both dog and owner. As with any other grooming technique, the first step is to identify the problem to be sure you have the right grooming tools and the time required to get the job done.

I use different methods for different matting situations, but what they all have in common is that they protect the dog's skin from getting scratched or, worse yet, cut by the de-matting tools. You should always hold the mat by the root near the skin with a gentle but firm grip that will buffer any pulling from reaching the root of the hair. This should be done on every mat, one at a time. Remember that hair is elastic, so the use of light leave-in conditioners will make the job easier.

Soft Mats

These mats are soft to the touch and usually can be separated by working them with your fingers. If you can open a hole in the middle of the mat and see through, **(1)** this kind of mat can be detangled by using a comb and a slicker brush. Holding the mat with one hand and using just the last tooth of the comb, begin to pull, or detangle, little by little starting at the outside edge of the mat (the farthest point from the skin) **(2)**. After you have opened a few sections, you can proceed to use a slicker brush, again working only on the edge of the mat **(3)**. Repeat this process in smaller sections, gradually moving deeper into the mat closer to the root.

A common mistake is skipping the comb step and using the slicker brush before the mats have been opened up. This will create a fur ball, which will damage the hair and tighten up the mat, making the whole process more difficult.

Use the tail of a rat-tail comb to open up a hole in the center of the mat.

After you open up a hole in the mat, use a comb to slowly detangle the hair.

Use a slicker brush to help work out the remaining tangles after, and only after, you have worked at the mat with a comb.

A matted dog is an uncomfortable dog. Approach each mat separately, holding the mat at its base, closest to the skin.

When using de-matting tools, always position your hand as a shield to protect the skin from the blades and to prevent from pulling the hair.

Depending on the type, cleanliness, and quality of the coat, different products can be applied to help the de-matting process.

On long-haired dogs, the use of a light leave-in conditioner containing cosmetic silicone will help to make the hair more manageable. Usually a little goes a long way, so always start by applying a small amount and repeating if necessary.

On dogs with medium double coats, sprinkling a small amount of cornstarch can help to loosen the packed undercoat.

Hard Mats

If the coat has turned into tight dreadlock-looking cords that can't be loosened with your fingers, a more drastic method is necessary. Cutting the mat with scissors parallel to the skin will break the "seal" and sometimes allow you to start detangling the mat using the end of the comb or a de-matting tool. It is crucial to remember that most de-matting tools have blades, so extra attention needs to be taken to be sure that neither the dog nor you gets hurt.

On long-haired dogs, the use of heavy de-matting solutions or a thick cream rinse can be used to soak up the matted area. Working the product into the coat with your fingers can, in some cases, loosen the mat.

Undercoats

The undercoat is a soft layer of coat present on double-coated dogs under a layer of harsher and thicker outer coat. The function of the undercoat is to protect the dog by insulating the body from extreme weather.

During winter months, the outer coat is the first barrier to stop wind and cold temperatures from reaching the soft undercoat layer that will act like a soft, fuzzy sweater keeping the body warm. During the summer months, dogs with double coats go through seasonal shedding because less undercoat is needed to allow fresh air to circulate under the outer coat—acting like the dog's own air conditioner unit protecting the body from overheating. Therefore, it is necessary to keep the undercoat properly brushed. Neglecting to keep double-coated dogs well brushed will cause the undercoat to get packed under the outer coat, causing the opposite effect: staying wet and cold in the winter and not allowing the air through in the summer.

When brushing the dog regularly, the use of a slicker brush and a wide-tooth comb will be enough. During shedding season, or when a dog is dropping a lot of undercoat—especially dogs with medium-length coats (who present thicker undercoats)—a wide-tooth comb and the eventual use of an undercoat rake will help to loosen the undercoat.

Remember that all de-shedding tools have blades. They will remove a lot of coat, but at the same time they will break the shaft of the outer coat, making it brittle and potentially changing the original texture, which makes it less effective at protecting the undercoat (and, in turn, protecting the dog's body). Nothing is better than a well-executed brushing routine to keep the coat healthy.

Once the undercoat has been loosened with the rake, use your slicker brush to finish the job.

CHAPTER 4

Bathing Your Dog

Bathing your dog generally will be the most physically demanding and potentially the messiest part of the grooming process, but it will also be one of the most important and rewarding moments because it will have both physical and emotional benefits.

Taking the time to rub your dog's hair and body while you are bathing him will feel as good to him as the best scalp massage at a top spa feels for you. Hair is surrounded by nerve endings and blood vessels, and the pleasure your dog will feel while you are massaging him will allow him to develop a real connection with you and make him feel relaxed and more comfortable about the grooming process to come.

When the hair is wet and a lot of the skin is exposed, check your dog for anything out of the ordinary such as cuts, bumps, scratches, fleas, and ticks. Just as we check our body in the shower to feel for any abnormalities that are not visible to the naked eye, while lathering your dog, apply the same attention by running your fingers along the entire body to feel for any growths or suspicious masses that could be growing under the skin. Applying gentle pressure with your fingers along the muscles and tendons will also help dogs relax and will relieve pain in older dogs or any dog that suffers from muscle or joint pain.

"Anybody who doesn't know what soap tastes like never washed a dog."
— *Franklin P. Jones*

Shampoo

My Shampoo, Your Shampoo, Our Shampoo?

It is not hard to realize that we are anatomically quite different from man's best friend, and that includes our hair.

We (human beings) have sweat glands all over our bodies, including our scalps. Sweating through our skin is one of the ways we get rid of toxins. Most dogs, on the other hand, or paw, only sweat through their tongues and pads and get rid of toxins by filtering them through their kidneys and excreting them in their feces. A dog's pH level is also different than ours (pH is a measurement of acidity in the body): a human's pH level is around 5.5, and a dog's is on average 7.5.

Because we sweat from our scalps, our shampoos have to be strong enough to remove toxins and oils that are released into the scalp. Because dogs do not sweat through their scalp and body, dog shampoo, which is much more gentle, is designed to penetrate the hair shaft and remove the dirt without stripping the coat of its natural oils. Dog hair is also more exposed to scratching and rubbing against hard surfaces than ours—this is the reason a dry coat will easily break.

If you run out of dog shampoo, you don't have to panic or leave your dog dirty. If you must use a human product, baby shampoo is the mildest shampoo with a similar pH balance. Use it, but be sure to add a good amount of conditioner so that the hair cuticle is properly nurtured and sealed.

Another fact to remember is that our skin is ten to fifteen cells thick, while your best friend's skin is only between three and five cell layers thick. This difference in thickness, therefore, makes your dog's skin more susceptible to harsher chemicals.

Choosing the Right Shampoo

We can divide shampoos into three main categories.

Regular Shampoo

This category can be divided into an endless list, but the basic ingredients don't vary much. Different additives will make them work better on white coats, dark coats, dry coats, and so on.

Natural anti-itch shampoos are included in this category because they use only natural ingredients, such as oatmeal, to add soothing properties.

Medicated Shampoo

We can group all shampoos with prescribed medicine in the medicated category. These types of products, available in most pet stores, should only be used under veterinary supervision. As good as tar and sulfur shampoos are to treat certain skin problems, they can cause serious problems to a dog with sensitive skin.

Flea and Tick Shampoo

There are various kinds of natural flea and tick shampoos on the market that are safe to use as a preventive bug repellent, especially for dogs that play outdoors a lot. If you must use chemical-based flea and tick shampoos, it is very important to take the necessary precautions to be sure that no shampoo gets inside the dog's eyes or mouth. The use of a protective ointment for the eyes is highly recommended when using any kind of shampoo other than a mild shampoo, and extreme caution should be used when applying the shampoo on the dog's head.

TIP

Following the manufacturer's dilution rate will make rinsing easier and help prevent skin reactions.

Cream Rinse and Conditioner

Depending on the coat, you can choose from different kinds of conditioners. Heavier conditioners are harder to rinse out, and most will leave a thicker coat on the hair, making them a perfect choice for long drop coats. Lighter conditioners will protect and coat the hair, adding minimum weight while helping to achieve a superfluffy look. Like shampoo, conditioners must be rinsed thoroughly unless the manufacturer's directions indicate a light rinse.

Leave-in Conditioner

These products are best used between baths or during daily brushing. Leave-in conditioners will add shine and flexibility to the hair and prevent breakage. For dogs with thick undercoats or very woolly coats, I recommend the use of a light leave-in conditioner to avoid product buildup. With these conditioners, a little product goes a long way. Using too much leave-in conditioner could turn your dog's coat into a dust magnet by making it sticky. Always start by applying a small amount; you can always add more if needed.

TIP

Elderly Dogs

When handling elderly dogs, it is very important to be sure that they are standing on a towel or a soft rubber mat where they will have a better grip to help them feel stable and secure. Slippery surfaces make dogs nervous, especially dogs of advanced age or those that have specific health issues, because their legs are not as strong as they once were.

Grooming and multitasking do not mix well. All your attention should be on your dog. For this reason, it is important to schedule the grooming for a time when you can work without being interrupted.

Setting Up a Location

You'll need to consider several factors to make grooming your dog both a safe and easy-to-clean-up experience. Because your full attention needs to be on the dog and grooming, you need to plan ahead to avoid interruptions. Every time you stop the action, the dog will feel like the job is done and he can go back to his daily routine. Focusing on the moment and keeping his concentration is important.

Choosing the right place to bathe your dog will depend on your dog's size and temperament. If you have a small dog that is accustomed to being handled and carried, you could bathe him in the kitchen sink, provided the dog fits comfortably in the sink and the faucet is dog friendly. The sink can easily become your washing station and the kitchen counter the perfect grooming area. For big and/or nervous dogs, the bathtub will be the safest bathing area.

Make a checklist of all the tools you will need to be sure that you won't have to leave your dog's side. Use a simple plastic caddy to have everything you need organized and easy to grab when you need it.

Observe the areas around the grooming space to figure out what could get wet and where the hair will fall to save you time and the risk of having a wet, soapy dog running loose. Most dogs think that running around wet is fun, but they are not aware that shampoo can make surfaces slippery, which can cause accidents.

The Bath

A thoroughly washed and properly dried coat will make the rest of the grooming much easier and the final result fabulous. Before you start the bath, your dog must already be properly brushed with all mats removed, ears cleaned, and nails cut. Cutting the nails before the bath will reduce the chances of cutting the quick. After the bath, the blood vessels will be dilated due to the warm temperature of the water, making the blood pressure build up inside the nails. Besides, if you happen to have a little blood on the nail, it's best to wash out the styptic powder used to stop the bleeding after a few minutes, preventing hair discoloration and any chance of your dog licking it. (Refer to "Trimming Nails" on page 80 for more information.)

Handling Your Dog

Place your dog in the tub on top of a nonslip surface. A loop leash or even an old leash around his neck will make the dog feel more comfortable by letting him know he can't or shouldn't go anywhere while being groomed. When on a leash, most dogs already know that they need to stay near you, so I like to use this trick during the bath. Some dogs react very quickly to a doorbell or a phone call, so having your dog on a leash will lower chances of him running out of the tub covered with soap and possibly becoming injured.

Water Temperature

Start by letting the water run so your dog can get used to the noise of the flowing water. Check the water temperature and make sure it is comfortable. Lukewarm is the perfect water temperature. We love long hot showers. Dogs don't.

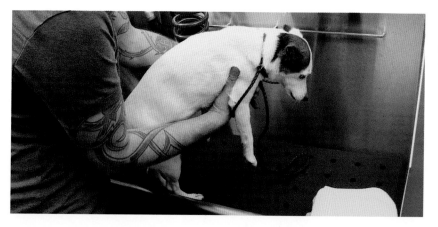

Placing a nonslip mat on the tub will help keep your dog relaxed.

Shampooing Your Dog

Wet the body first and leave the head for later, as many dogs panic when water is poured over their head. Make sure your dog is as calm as possible before slowly starting to wet his head. Keeping your dog's head tilted slightly upward while running the water over his head will help prevent water from getting into his nose. **(1)**

The best way to bathe your dog is to start by applying shampoo on the dirtiest areas first (such as paws, privates, and belly) to be sure that the shampoo has extra time to work its way into the coat for deep cleaning. **(2)**

The head and face should be the last areas to get wet and shampooed and the first ones to be rinsed, to avoid excessive shaking and fewer chances for the shampoo to get in the eyes, ears, and mouth.

With the help of the correct size bathing brush, start by gently scrubbing the bottom of the paws, making sure no dirt is left in between the pads and the nails. With the coat wet, closely examine the skin for fleas, ticks, cuts, scratches, or any other skin abnormalities. **(3)**

This is a good time to check your dog's anal glands because all the secretions will flush down the drain with the bath. (To learn more, refer to "Anal Glands" at the end of this chapter.)

Once the body is perfectly scrubbed, move on to the head. While holding your dog's head with both of your hands, kiss his nose and assure him that both of you are doing a great job.

Use your free hand to tilt your dog's head back so water doesn't run into his nose.

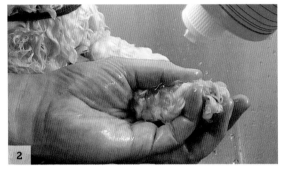

Head straight for where your dog is dirtiest, the paws and belly.

In the bath, when the hair is wet, is a great time to check for any skin issues. Spotting any changes or abnormalities is one of the reasons I believe regular grooming for a dog is so important.

Face

How often should you clean your dog's face? This is one of the questions I am most frequently asked. To which I respond with a question of my own: How often do you wash your own face?

Try placing yourself in your dog's shoes, or paws, for a while: shoving your face into a bowl of food and having only your tongue for a napkin; sitting on a curb or walking on the sidewalk with all the car fumes, dust, and debris of the city being swept right into your face; or running in the park on all fours with all the dirt from the ground blowing into your eyes. Add to this the fact that a dog's face is often the area most neglected by owners during bathing for fear of getting soap and water into their pet's eyes, ears, and mouths and what do you get? A constantly dirty face.

For these reasons, and many others, you should try to clean your dog's face as often as possible. Make it a point to wash your dog's face every time you bathe him, and also make it part of your daily routine to give his face a quick wipe with a moist paper towel or a wet wipe after each walk outside or run in the park. Again, the head should be the last area to get wet and shampooed and the first area to be rinsed in order to avoid excessive shaking and fewer chances for the shampoo to get into the eyes, ears, and mouth.

The Process

Start by scrubbing and massaging the ear flaps with your fingers to help remove any extra oils that have accumulated. While gently holding the head, with the help of a wet washcloth or a small face brush or comb, clean around his eyes, forehead, and chin. Even though special attention should be given to dogs with flat wrinkled faces (like bulldogs or pugs) or dogs with short muzzles and bright eyes (like shih tzus or Maltese), all dogs can benefit from a few basic cleaning steps to prevent a bacteria-welcoming environment that will result in tearstains.

A washcloth is the best way to gently scrub away dirt from your dog's face without getting shampoo in his eyes. Pay close attention to all the folds of your dog's face around the lips and chin where food and dirt can easily accumulate. Dirt in between the folds can allow bacteria to grow, be a source of bad odor, and lead to discoloration of the hair in that area. Be sure to carefully wash the top of the nose—because we all know that dogs have the habit of sticking their noses into everything.

Stains

The cause of most tear or face stains is bacteria growth in areas that are constantly wet. Also, while small dogs are growing and teething, their skull bones can often shift and their gums can get inflamed causing their small tear ducts to move and get misaligned. This misalignment of the tear ducts will not allow the tears to reach the eyeballs, triggering the production of extra tears and more moisture and thus tearstains.

On dogs with flat faces, tears may not be the only problem. Water from the bowl or saliva from playing with an overly wet plush toy can cause humidity to collect in between the folds and create a bacteria-friendly environment.

The first step of stain removal is to identify the source and nip it in the bud. Your approach can be external, internal, or a combination of both. There are plenty of pet store products, but none of them will work if you don't take care of the root of the problem first.

Dogs like to stick their noses in the most unusual places; special attention needs to be paid to the face when bathing a dog.

Eyes

Externally, always try to keep the eye area clean by using solutions and eye wipes specifically designed for tearstains. The use of powders near the eye area will help from a cosmetic point of view, but it could irritate the eyes, making your dog produce extra tears. Some pet products have a small amount of antibiotics, so be sure to consult with your vet before you start treating your dog with these products.

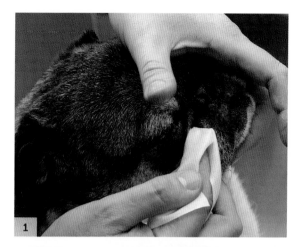

Clean your dog's eyes with lint-free cotton balls, cotton pads, wipes, or paper towels. **(1)** Never scrub while the coat is dry, which can make matters worse by scratching and irritating the area. If your dog has been playing in the sand or in a very dusty area, flush his eyes with an eyewash solution before you wipe. **(2)** A plastic flea comb can help you safely comb out sand from the eye area.

It doesn't take much sand or debris to clog the tear ducts and make your dog very uncomfortable. This often triggers them to scratch their faces by rubbing them on the carpet, grass, or—even worse—the street, exposing them to serious eye injuries.

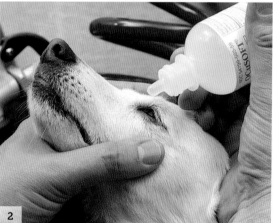

An internal approach, which requires changing the pH of the saliva and tears, has proven very successful. This can be achieved by supplementing the dog's food or water with an alkaline agent such as calcium, potassium, or organic apple vinegar, which will help to stop the growth of bacteria.

Regardless of whether you saw any shampoo drip into the eyes or not, it is a good safety measure to rinse the eyes with a plain eyewash solution.

If necessary, follow up with a second shampooing, which will leave the coat squeaky clean, making it easier to trim. This is especially helpful for dogs with extremely oily coats and dogs that get very dirty.

Ears

Proper ear cleaning should always start with a thorough examination of both ears.

Look

A visual examination will identify any abnormalities such as the following:

- Redness
- Inflammation
- Abscesses
- Scratches
- Excess hair obstructing the ear canal
- Parasites

Smell

Smelling your dog's ears will also help identify anything out of the ordinary. The inside of a healthy ear should smell like the rest of the dog. Any strong and/or unpleasant odor is a clear indication that something is wrong. If after inspection the ears appear to be healthy, you may begin cleaning them.

The ear canal should look clean, open, and be the same color as the ear flap. If it looks puffy and red like an angry man's face, it is time to visit the vet.

Dogs know better than anybody about the power of a sniff. Any strong smell should lift a red flag and warrant a trip to the vet's office.

Soak a cotton ball in an ear cleaning solution made for dogs. Place the cotton ball in the ear canal and gently massage the ear, making the dog feel he is just getting a head rub. During this massage, also gently remove dirt from the ear. **(1)**

After you release the ears, your dog will probably instinctively shake his head. It is a good idea to move your head away to give him room to shake-shake-shake. Accidents can easily happen in the shower or tub, so always hold your dog to prevent him from slipping in the tub and hurting himself, especially when he is shaking.

If necessary, repeat the ear cleaning process to be sure all the dirt and accumulated wax is removed.

Thoroughly rinse the area around the ear, either by gently covering the ear canal with your thumb to avoid getting water into the canal or by folding the ear down and spraying the dog with water from above. Always make sure that water does not enter the ear canal. **(2)**

After the bath, add a couple drops of ear cleaner to change the pH level from any humidity left inside the ear canal, which will deter the growth of any future bacteria.

If the ear seems infected (you'll smell a strong odor), consult with your veterinarian to identify the correct product to use.

If you used cotton balls to protect the dog's ear canal, this is a good time to remove them and apply a few drops of ear cleaning solution to avoid any possibility of humidity accumulation. **(3)**

Make sure to use ear cleaning solution made for dogs.

Rubbing the solution-soaked cotton inside the ear canal can feel just as good as a tummy rub.

Always be sure to remove the cotton ball from the ears after the grooming is finished. I have seen cotton balls that have been left behind for weeks!

Wash

When Bathing

Remember that the skin inside a dog's ear is very delicate and because dogs' hearing is so sensitive, they get particularly nervous when you try to clean them.

Cotton balls serve a dual purpose and are the best and most gentle way to clean the ears. You should place dry cotton balls inside the ears when bathing your dog to make sure that water doesn't enter the ear canals. Water inside a dog's ear can lead to infections and cause serious problems. This is especially true for dogs with dropped or folded ears. Even though a healthy ear can be safely washed without cotton balls, as a safety measure it is always better to use them.

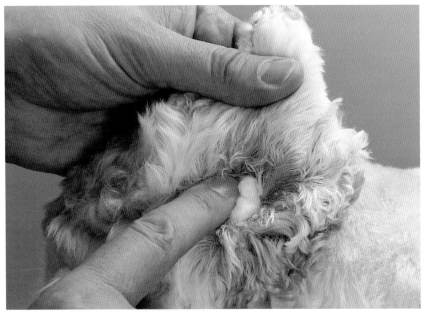

Gently place a dry cotton ball in each ear to act as a water barrier during bathing.

Excess Hair

If your dog has excess hair in the ears, you can gently remove the hair with your fingers or a hemostat tool. First, hold the ear open and apply some ear powder to make the hair easy to pull. **(1)**

Then, with a soft but firm hand, pinch the excess and possibly knotted hair with the fingers of the other hand and gently pull a few hairs at a time. **(2)**

If the hair in and/or around the ears is very oily, apply cornstarch or baby powder and let it sit for a few minutes before cleaning the ear. **(3)**

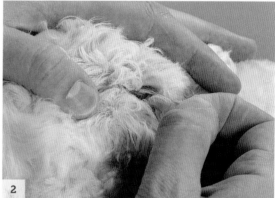

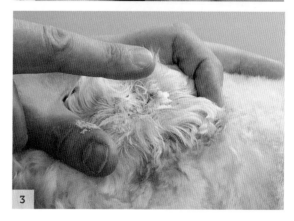

Rinsing

The dirtiest parts of the dog are the parts closest to the ground: the paws and belly. By rinsing in a head-to-tail, top-to-bottom direction, you keep the dirtiest water from washing over the cleaner areas. Use your free hand to move and massage the coat as you rinse, making sure the water penetrates to the skin and that the soap rinses out completely. Keep rinsing until the water rinses out clean. Shampoo left on your dog can cause itching or irritation of the skin.

Conditioning

Now that the coat has been properly shampooed and rinsed, it is time to apply the conditioner. Most breeds will benefit from the application of conditioner. Dogs with wiry coats, such as Jack Russells, Airedale terriers, and other dogs with similar coats, can get away with just a good shampoo and no conditioner. Most others breeds, especially breeds with long and soft coats, require conditioner. Shampoo companies have invested a lot of time and money developing their products. For this reason, make sure to read and follow the manufacturer's directions for optimal results. Overdiluted products will not deliver good results.

When we rinse off in the shower, the water runs from head to toe, which is just what you want to do when rinsing your dog head to paw.

Massaging your dog while rinsing will help keep your dog calm and ensure a more thorough rinse of the coat and skin.

Teeth

It is okay if your dog's breath doesn't smell like roses, but if you have to hold your breath when your dog tries to kiss you, it is probably a sign that something is wrong. The difference between doggie breath and an unhealthy mouth is pretty clear. Also, because breath can be a sign of more serious mouth problems, it is a good idea to use this opportunity to take a closer look and check for any abnormalities inside and outside the mouth. A daily checkup of just lifting the dog's lips to check his gums and pearly whites is the best way of detecting many dental problems early on. This will save your dog from a great deal of discomfort and will ultimately save you money on vet bills.

Ideally, you should brush your dog's teeth every day, but if you haven't trained your dog from a young age, you, like many others, might prefer to give in to his sad puppy face and brush his teeth infrequently. This might not be a deal breaker if you give him special dental toys or treats that can often help control the situation.

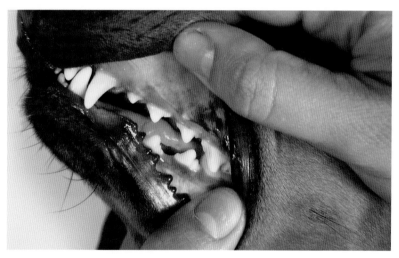

Training your dog for beauty includes getting him used to having his teeth brushed from an early age.

Toothbrushes come in a variety of shapes and sizes. Some are shaped like our own toothbrushes, and others are made to fit around your finger. A clean piece of gauze wrapped around your finger will sometimes work just as well. The regular use of dental gels will prevent the growth of bacteria and tartar buildup.

Never use human toothpaste or oral rinses on your dog because it could make him sick and be toxic. Human products are made to be spit out. Unless your dog is an Internet sensation, I doubt that he will know how to spit out the leftover toothpaste. Human dental products also contain fluoride that, when ingested, can make your dog sick. Pet stores offer large selections of dental hygiene products made especially for dogs.

Most of the tartar buildup occurs on the outside of the dog's teeth, so it is not necessary to brush the insides of the teeth very often.

Poor dental hygiene doesn't just affect your dog's breath. The buildup of tartar will corrode the surface of the teeth and will allow the bacteria to find its way into the bloodstream, exposing your dog to heart, liver, and kidney diseases.

Most dental diseases originate on the gums. Therefore, it is important to constantly check them. Any excessive redness or inflammation is a clear sign that you need to take your dog to the vet and have them checked out.

Remember that your dog trusts you more than anybody else. When possible, be proactive at the vet's office and help hold your dog—but only if your presence will not make things worse.

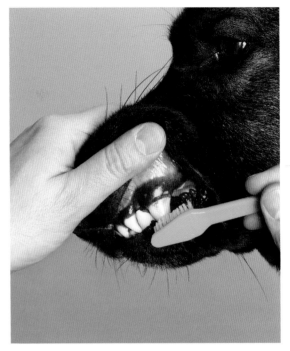

While gently lifting the dog's lip, use a circular motion to soften up and remove the food stuck on and between teeth.

Flavored toothpaste will make it easier when it is time to reach for the molars.

Anal Glands

I know how much we love to celebrate every trick our best friend does, but if you see your dog scooting across the living room area rug, it's not only time to call the carpet cleaners, but it's also time to address the issue of your best friend's anal glands.

Anal glands, or anal sacs, are filled with a very smelly fluid that dogs use to mark their territory and identify others. These glands served a purpose back in the day when the ancestors of today's dogs ran around in packs. After diets changed to easy-to-digest processed foods like the ones we feed our dogs today, the consistency of their stool also changed. Anal glands release naturally when dogs defecate. If the glands don't get enough pressure or stimulation, though, especially with dogs who suffer from excessively loose stool, they may not empty completely. If a dog is chewing, licking, or dragging his bottom after he goes to the bathroom, this indicates that the glands have fluid in them, they are irritated, and they may need to be expressed.

The sacs are located in the four o'clock and eight o'clock positions on the dog's anus. This procedure is better done before the bath, inside the tub, because the released fluids could spray out from the pressure. If the area is very red, it is best to take your dog to the vet to get it done.

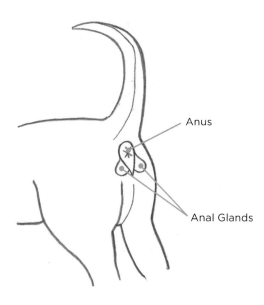

Anus

Anal Glands

After warming the area with running water or a wet paper towel, position the paper towel (or a few of them) over the anus area. Use one hand to hold your dog's tail up and use the other hand to locate the glands. These glands, when full, will feel like a couple of peas.

Position your fingers below the glands and apply a gentle but constant pressure in the form of a pinch. Most likely, your dog will strain, tensing his rectal muscles. Pushing your fingers in the direction of the glands, keep steady pressure and let nature do its work.

It is not unusual that only one gland is affected, so it is important to assess the situation when getting ready.

After the glands have released their fluid, it is a good idea to quickly rinse out the tub before your dog steps in any of the mess. The fluid released should be similar in color to the dog's normal stool and have a soft to semisoft consistency. It is normal that the first secretion is more dense than the rest because it has been sitting there the longest. Glands filled with a very thick fluid should be monitored closely. If you notice that the dog continues to feel uncomfortable or that the chewing or licking of the area or butt dragging continues or gets worse, it might be a good idea to have the glands checked by the vet to be sure they are not infected.

You can try to avoid the frequency of the problem or avoid the problem altogether by choosing the right diet for your dog. A high-quality dog food that keeps the stool firm will help your dog to naturally release the anal glands during bowel movements.

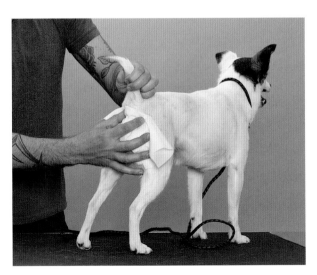

Your dog's anal glands are located at the four and eight o' clock position of the anus, and for some dogs, will occasionally require expression.

	TOWEL DRY	HIGH-VELOCITY DRYER	FLUFF DRY
Short Hair	●	●	
Medium to Thick Hair	●	●	
Long Hair	●		●

Drying

Use different drying techniques depending on your dog's size and the type and length of coat it has. It is important to mention here that if you plan to trim your dog's hair, the coat must be completely dry before doing any trimming.

Burrito Wrap

A towel dry is the first step and should be done while the dog is still in the tub. Wrapping your dog in what I call a "burrito wrap" is not only soothing for your best friend but also gives you a firm grip to safely transport your dog to the work area.

The best way to wrap the dog in a towel is to first cover your hand with one end of the towel. Position this hand under the dog, going under his belly and through his hind legs. With this hand, gently lift the dog a few inches from the tub and with your other free hand, wrap the dog with the towel going over and under. Now that you are in control, slide the "wrapped" hand out and lift the dog. He will be comfortable and secure.

Letting your dog rest a few minutes in the burrito wrap will give the hair cuticle enough time to seal and absorb all of the shampoo's nutrients inside the hair shaft. If your dog is too big, or too anxious, to be carried like a wrapped baby around the house, keeping the dog in his cage or a confined area with a couple of towels under him will do the trick.

Hugging a dripping wet dog is not always a good idea. Your dog will welcome a nice warm hug while wrapped in the comfort of a soft towel. The burrito wrap can make lifting your dog out of the tub easier and make him feel secure.

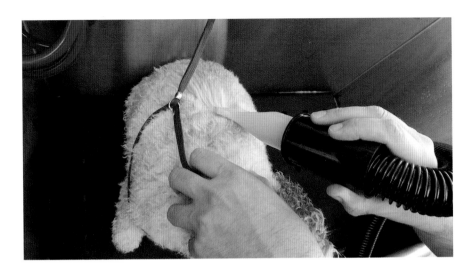

Blow Dry

Rushing to blow-dry the hair will result in drying out the nutrients before they have had the chance to penetrate, leaving the hair excessively dry and brittle and prone to breakage. Well-nurtured hair will also help keep the style in good shape much longer.

For dogs with short or medium-length coats with or without undercoat, such as Jack Russells or golden retrievers, a towel dry followed by a high-velocity hair dryer to dry and remove dead coat and undercoat is recommended. A high-velocity dryer, also known as a force-dryer, is one of the professional dog groomer's secret weapons.

High-velocity dryers come in various shapes, sizes, and powers. Most high-velocity dryers are noisy. For nervous dogs, using cotton balls in the ears or wrapping a scarf or towel around the head to cover the ears will make them feel more at ease.

When using any kind of dryer, it is important to first turn it on pointing away from your dog to give him a few seconds to get used to the noise and then slowly approach the dog with the dryer.

When using a high-velocity dryer, it is important to sweep the water from the back of the head to the tail and down the sides to avoid rewetting areas that you have already dried. High-velocity dryers will get your dog almost dry. In summer months, a walk outside will be enough to completely dry his coat.

A blow dryer holder works by blowing warm air in the direction you want while leaving your hands free to work.

Brush and dry in the direction the hair grows on a dog with a drop coat, such as a shi tzu or maltese.

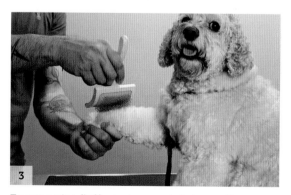

To get a nice fluffy coat on curly hair, use the brush and blow dryer air stream to go against the direction of hair growth.

Fluff Drying

Fluff-drying is done on the table with a handheld blow dryer. It is important to remember that the air temperature must be kept to its minimum heat setting to avoid burning the skin and damaging the coat. A blow dryer holder (available from pet stores or improvised) will free up both of your hands to hold the dog and brush under the stream of warm air. **(1)**

The direction that you blow-dry will alter the end results. Dogs with drop coats, such as Yorkshires, Maltese, shih tzus, or cocker spaniels, should be fluff-dried in the direction that the hair grows to achieve a neat finish with minimum flyaway hairs. **(2)** For fluffy-looking dogs, such as bichons frises or poodle-type breeds, brushing under the dryer against the grain will lift all the hair up, making it much easier to trim. **(3)**

Ear flaps and skin folds are especially delicate when exposed to heat. Be extra cautious when drying these areas.

Never point a dryer directly into your dog's face. Always dry these areas directing the air from the top or behind. Remember, dogs are very sensitive!

Sponge Bath Technique

A sponge bath is a great way to clean the areas of the dog that need it when a traditional bath is not an option and a dry bath is not enough.

For sponge baths, the use of a waterless, or self-rinse, shampoo is the best option. Self-rinse shampoo is designed to clean and leave minimum residue on the dog.

Start by removing dirt, food, or anything else that needs to be washed out using a paper towel or, even better, wet wipes. If available, use dog wipes, which are usually thicker and soaked with more cleaning solution than wipes made for humans.
Dog wipes are good not only for spot cleaning but for removing dust that accumulates on the dog's coat after a fun day at the park.

After you have removed (with the help of dog wipes or paper towels) as much dirt as you can, soak a washcloth or a sponge in self-rinse shampoo. Grabbing a section of the dirty hair from the root, slide your hand down, removing the dirt with the washcloth or sponge. Repeat this process always using a clean section of the rag or by rinsing it and starting again. After all the dirty areas have been treated with self-rinse shampoo, go over them again with a washcloth dampened with the same self-rinse shampoo, but this time dilute the shampoo with water (one part shampoo to one part water). This way, you will remove any dirt left behind and not leave as much of the self-rinse product on the dog.

Finish by towel-drying the area with a dry towel and brush it to allow air to circulate and better dry the area, especially if a hair dryer is not available.

Having the products and tools for a quick sponge bath with you can become very handy on bumpy rides that could result in some motion sickness accidents.

After towel drying the area, be sure to brush the coat to avoid matting the hair.

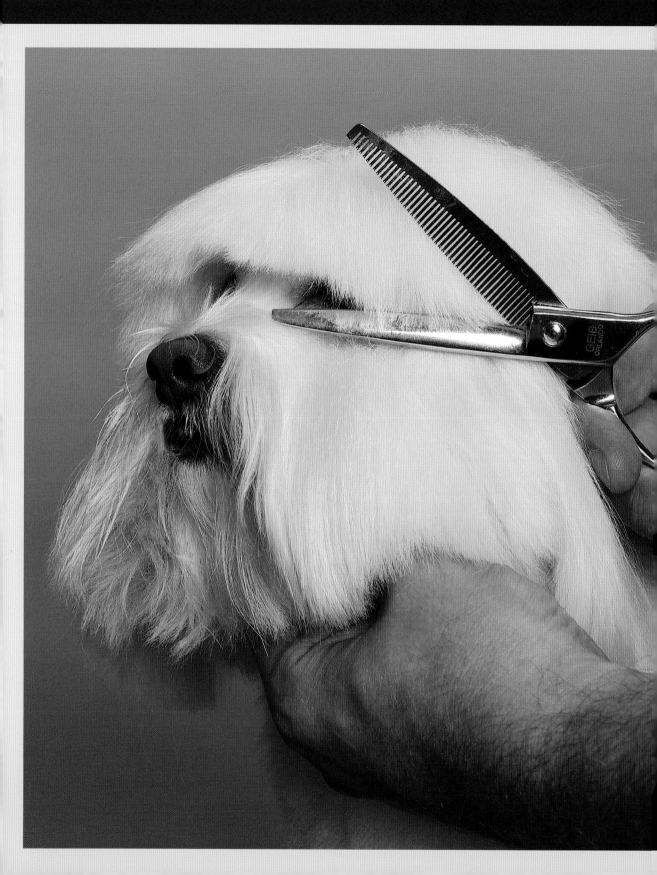

CHAPTER 5

Trimming

Although a standard trim is the most involved part of the grooming process, it is also when you will express your creativity and individuality the most. You should have a clear and planned-out idea of what you are trying to achieve before you begin any trimming. Improvising can often lead to disaster. Being prepared will produce a better result all around. It will save you time and, more important, minimize the amount of time your dog will be inconvenienced.

Quick trims can also come in handy. A last-minute photo opportunity, a sudden trip out of town, or just a sanitary "bikini" or face trim are all instances that could benefit from a few quick touch-ups when your regular groomer is not available or when you are planning to stretch the time between grooming salon visits a couple of extra weeks. A well-executed light trim will go a long way to refreshing a slightly overgrown haircut.

On more than one occasion I have been contacted for a last-minute television segment with my dog when I had only a few minutes to get him ready. Trimming just his face and feet was all it took to make him look freshly groomed, and nobody could see that the hair under his t-shirt was long and scruffy.

Basic trimming techniques apply equally to most all dogs and are the best "tools" for early detection of many health issues.

Trimming Nails

Before clipping a dog's nails, it is important to understand how the nails are constructed. The very tip of the nail (the hollow part) is the safest and, in my opinion, only place for a home groomer to cut. For white nails, you can identify the tip by holding the nail up to the light and locating the whitest part of the nail. Darker nails require a closer look. You can identify the cuttable tip part of a dark nail by looking at the nail from the bottom and finding the hollow, veinless tip. Beyond the tip of the nail is the main body of the nail, which also contains the vein commonly called the quick.

Clipping the nail as close as possible to the quick will force the vein to recede and make subsequent nail clipping much easier. Be very careful to cut only the tip of the nail. If the nail is very long, you will have to repeat this process weekly until you reach the desired length. Do not cut past the quick line to avoid bleeding. If the quick is slightly cut as a mishap and the nail bleeds, do not freak out. Pinch some styptic powder between your fingers and apply and hold the powder with gentle pressure to the tip of the nail until the bleeding stops.

A good time to clip the nails is at the beginning of the grooming session. When the dog starts to get anxious or too happy, his blood pressure will naturally rise, pushing the blood harder into the veins inside the nails and making them more exposed. Some groomers like to clip the nails after the bath because they are softer, but in my opinion, the warm water will not

On dogs with long hair, it is a good idea to cover the paw with a piece of kitchen-grade stretch film. Let the nails poke through and pull back the film, which will keep the hair out of the way and expose the nails making them easier to clip.

Nails can be filed after cutting to smooth out sharp edges.

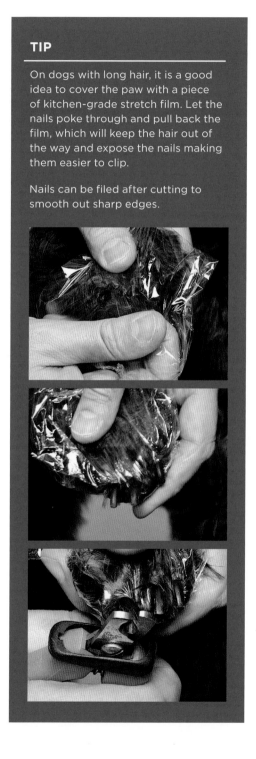

only soften the nail but dilate the blood vessels as well. My advice is to get it out of the way first and then move on to more fun stuff.

To make the job less stressful and a more successful experience for you and your dog, handle the dog correctly while clipping the nails with a soft but firm touch, always making sure to hold the paw in a comfortable position. Pulling his paw in an unnatural or uncomfortable position will turn a nail-clipping experience into tug-of-war. Remember, we are dancing, not playing tug-of-war. If the dog is pulling his paw, it means he is scared, nervous, or uncomfortable.

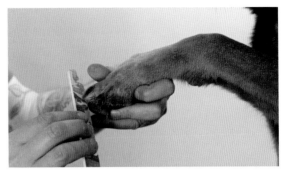

Your dog can enjoy a spa treatment just like you, and filing down nails after a nail trim has left them sharp helps them not scratch or catch on anything.

My preferred nail trimming tool, which I divulged in chapter two, is the plier-shaped trimmer.

Use a firm, yet gentle, hold on the paw so that you can easily trim the tip of the nail. Your dog will feel more comfortable if you act with confidence.

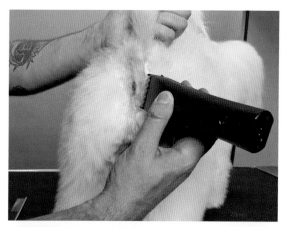

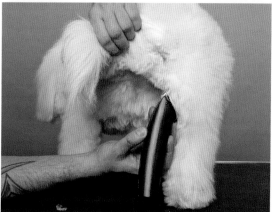

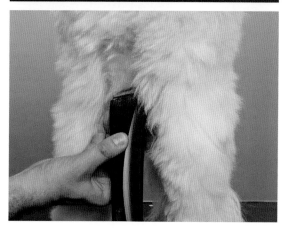

Sanitary Trimming

Sometimes, keeping your dog's private areas neatly trimmed can be enough to get you by between grooming appointments or when your dog groomer is on vacation.

A dog's private areas are very sensitive and many dogs don't enjoy you being all up in their business. So, it is necessary to be extra careful when grooming these areas. Moreover, a dog's genital areas are often hard to reach and any sudden movement can be dangerous, especially when you are handling clippers.

When trimming the perianal area, be sure to point the clipper outward and avoid touching this skin with the blade.

The easiest way to trim your dog's genital areas is to gently lift one of the back legs, clip one side, and then repeat the process on the other side while lifting the other leg.

Most small cordless trimmers do not offer a blade that is suitable for clipping the private areas because the hair will be left too short, possibly causing irritation. To safely trim your dog's genital and perianal areas, use a #10 blade. It will leave ¹⁄₁₆ inch (1.6 mm) of hair. Holding the dog upright will give you a clean visual and help keep the skin tight to avoid scratching the folds and wrinkles.

Clipping these areas shorter than that could irritate the dog's skin, and using a blade that would leave a longer hair length could result in cutting the skin because the blade teeth are more separated.

Trimming Pads and Feet

As explained in chapter 1, dog's paws are very sensitive and need to be handled gently. Most dogs will react by pulling back or suddenly jerking when they feel that you are pulling the leg in an uncomfortable position. This is why it is important to encourage the dog to rest his paw in your hand. This gives him time to readjust his weight and balance and feel stable by relying on the support of his other legs. Once the dog is relaxed, start with a gentle massage-like motion to inspect and then lead the paw into the correct position needed to trim the paws.

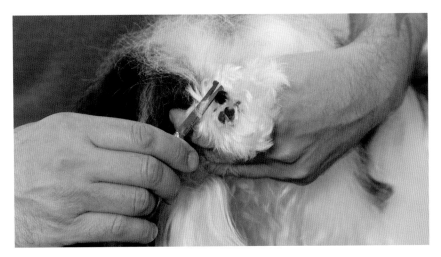

Gently pulling the leg up in a natural position will help you trim the pads without stressing your dog.

Basic Paw Trim

Dogs with medium or long hair tend to grow an excessive amount of hair between the pads. Keeping the pads free of this hair will make it harder for debris and foreign objects to get stuck between the dog's paws, which could make it uncomfortable and sometimes dangerous for the dog.

The use of small round-tip scissors is a safe way to trim the extra hair between the pads. Don't go too deep, as the skin between the pads is very thin and sensitive. Clipping the hair flush with the pads will keep the area clean. If you prefer to use clippers, you should not dig in between the pads in order to avoid scratching the delicate skin.

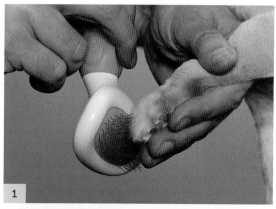

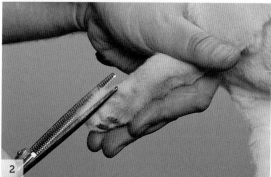

Dogs with Medium Coats

On dogs with a medium-length coat, the best way to trim the extra hair on top of the paw between the toes is by using a slicker brush and thinning shears.

Start by holding the paw in the palm of your hand. Lift the hair between the toes with a slicker brush **(1)** and then trim all the hair that stands up with the thinning shears. **(2)** Avoid getting too close to the top of the toes to achieve a natural look. Follow by brushing the hair down and then up again and with the help of your fingers, be sure no long hairs are curled in between the toes. Go over the area one more time with the thinning shears before putting the dog's paw down. While trimming the hair with thinning shears, always be careful not to scratch your dog's skinny knuckles.

Once the dog is standing in his natural position, use small curved scissors to go around the paw trimming all the hair that touches the floor. **(3)** With the help of a comb, move the hair around in different directions and trim the excess hair to get a clean finished look.

This is the best way to trim golden retrievers, long-haired Chihuahuas, Pomeranians, and so on.

Dogs with Long Coats

After trimming the hair between the pads, while the dog is standing in a natural position with the hair brushed down neatly, gently wrap your hand around his leg right above the paw and then move your hand down until you reach 1 inch (2.5 cm) above the floor. Carefully lift the paw and bend it backward following the natural movement of the leg. At this point you should have a clear view of the already clean pads. With curved scissors, trim the hair following the shape of the pads. Keep the scissors at a slight angle to achieve a beveled shape. **(1)**

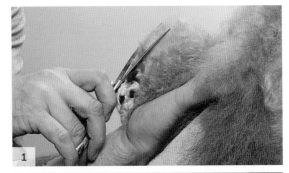

With the dog standing in his natural position, trim around the paws, keeping the scissors at a 45-degree angle to neaten up the paws. **(2)**

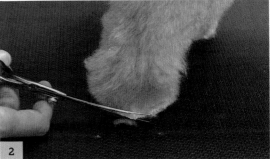

Slightly lifting the paw, trim the edges to blend the top of the feet. Be careful not to go too short on top of the paw because you will have to blend it later with the rest of the leg. You can always take more hair off later, but you can't add hair that is already gone. **(3)**

Finish by going over the whole paw with thinning shears to erase any scissors marks and smooth out the edges. **(4)**

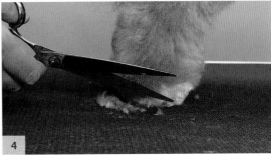

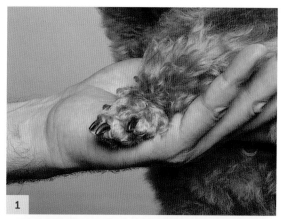

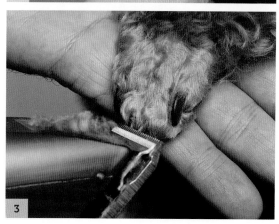

Clean (or Shaved) Feet

This style is mostly used on poodles, but it has become popular on long-haired dogs that live in the city as a way to keep their feet clean. Not all dogs can sport "clean" feet; some dogs have very sensitive skin and clipping the feet short could trigger them to start licking and irritating the area. Applying a small quantity of an aloe vera–based lotion after trimming the feet short may help relieve the irritation.

Start by gently leading your dog to position his paw in the palm of your hand and then slowly proceed to slide your hand down until you have a firm grip of the dog's paw. Remember the Tango Theory. **(1)** While the dog's paw is resting on the palm of your hand, move the hair from the bottom of the leg up to have a clear visual of the feet to avoid cutting leg hair.

With a small trimmer or your clippers using the #15 or #30 blade, begin by trimming the hair on the bottom of the paws. Pay extra attention because the skin between the toes is thin and very sensitive. **(2)**

Carefully clip the hair between the dog's toes. Use small strokes and lift the hair between the toes by sliding your fingers against the direction of the hair growth. **(3)**

Small trimmers are great for this job because they are very quiet and do not vibrate as much, making it easy to work around very sensitive areas.

Trimming Heads and Faces

It is no secret that a cute dog face can make even the most hardened individual smile.

Your dog's personality and individual sense of style can help you decide on the perfect trim. The following are general guidelines for trimming heads and faces. Your creativity plays an important role. Experimenting with different lengths will give you different looks. Remember, it's really about expressing yourself.

It helps to visualize the head in three sections: the top of the skull, from the occiput to the eyebrow line **(1)**; the sides of the head or cheek area, from under the ear to the outside corner of the eye and down the jawline **(2)**; and the chin area, from the chin to the Adam's apple. **(3)**

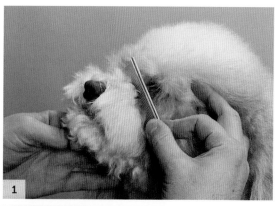

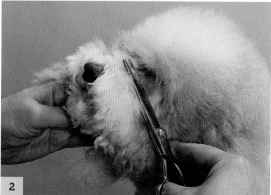

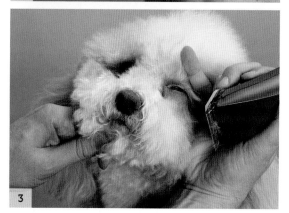

Around the Eyes

Start by trimming the hair between your dog's eyes.

This will open up his expression and make him feel more comfortable because he won't have any hair covering his eyes. Start by using a small comb to lift the hair from the inside corner of the eyes using an outward and upward motion. **(1)** Because this area is most prone to tearstains, keeping the hair short will help reduce the problem. Either with a pair of small round-tip scissors or with thinning shears—always pointing forward or away from the dog's eyes to avoid any accident resulting from your pet's unexpected movement—trim the hair around the eyes. **(2)**

This area can also be trimmed with clippers using a #10 blade. Clippers will trim closer than a pair of scissors, but because most dogs don't feel comfortable having vibrating clippers so close to their face, chances are you will have to use scissors. Hair around the eyes should be kept trimmed, especially for dogs with recurring eye problems. **(3)**

The steps for trimming around your dog's eyes remain the same regardless of hair type.

Note that small changes on the holding pressure with your free hand will keep the dog's focus away from the tools.

Dogs feel our adrenaline through our breath; popping a mint will help disguise any anxiety while working on delicate areas. I find that whispering happy songs helps relax both me and the dog while trimming the face.

Round Face (for Flat Coats)

Top of Head and Face

Whether you're using scissors or clippers with an attachment comb, the steps to create a nice round face and head are the same, regardless of whether or not your dog's coat is flat or curly.

Start by combing forward the hair on top of the head.

For flat coats, use your clippers with the medium length attachment comb. This will leave approximately 1 inch (2.5 cm) of hair, which will still be fluffy but short enough to last a few weeks without growing into the face too quickly.

Clip from the occiput to the eyebrows. When doing this, be careful not to cut the hair from the top of his ears. **(1)**

Blend the top of the head with the ears with the help of thinning shears.

Then, holding the ears up, either with your hand or a hair clip, use the same attachment comb to clip down the sides of the head. **(2)**

Lift the chin up and clip down the dog's neck to the Adam's apple. To achieve a sweet look don't leave much hair under the chin. Keeping the chin short will help to keep the face cleaner. **(3)** Remember this is the dirtiest part of the face.

Comb all the hair forward again and go over with the clippers one more time following the same process.

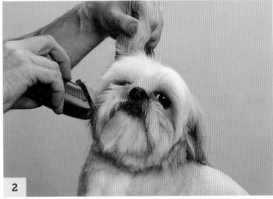

4

5

6

Holding the ears forward, trim the hair behind the ears in both directions and blend the top of the head to the neck, clipping the hair from the occiput down to the neck. **(4)**

Connect the nose to the inside of the ears to create a half-moon line that follows the jawline. **(5)**

Now connect the dots and blend all the edges. **(6)** We almost know how to do this instinctively because of our own experiences during our lifetime of having our hair cut. I'm sure you've seen your hairstylist cut your hair section by section and then check his or her work to make sure that all the sides are even and connected and that there are no stray hairs. Many times they repeat sections to make sure everything is just right.

A practical way to choose the right length of the ears is to pull the ears forward and trim the hair that passes the nose. This will not only make the ears look fabulous but also prevent them from getting dirty from food or the floor.

Finish by trimming the bottom of the ears by holding the ear tip and its hair flat in between your fingers. Place your fingers just beyond the tip of the ear flaps and hold them there. By doing so, your fingers will protect the edges of the ear flaps by stopping the scissors so that it will only cut the hair and not the skin of the ear flaps. Positioning the blade of the shears at a 45-degree angle will help you create a clean beveled edge.

Round Face Using Scissors

Imagine a circle around the dog's head with his eyes at the center. Comb the hair at the top of this circle up and use curved shears to trim the top of the head, forming a semicircle from ear to ear. You may need to use a little bit of hairspray to help hold the hair in place while you trim it.

Comb forward the hair on top of his head and use your thinning shears to shape the dog's visor. Start by using scissors from the outside corner of the eye always pointing the scissors toward the nose on both sides. This will open up the dog's expression and avoid the hair from falling into his face.

Follow this by trimming the front of the bangs with the scissors at a 45-degree angle to create a beveled effect. Comb forward and trim the hair between the eyes to avoid a "horned" look.

With the thinning shears pointing forward for safety, cut following an imaginary line connecting the outside corner of the eye to the tip of the nose. The use of thinning shears will give the dog a much softer look. After both sides are done, trim the front area to give it a softer, more rounded shape. **(1)**

Following the jawline using an imaginary half-moon curve, connect the tip of the chin with the base of the ear. Folding the ear flap over the head will keep it out of the way. **(2)**

Comb the hair up and out from the cheeks and trim it following a neat line that will help connect the side of the head with the top of the head.

Use thinning shears to blend the top of the head with the top of the ears. **(3)** Pull the ear forward and trim the hair behind the ear to blend it with the neck.

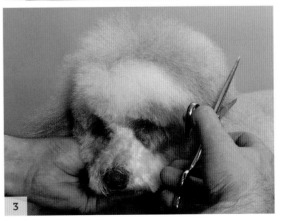

Long Hair Variations

Trim the hair on the bottom of the ears using your fingers as a guide. **(1)** Check your work by combing the already-cut hair in different directions to be sure no hair is sticking out. Finish by combing the hair in different directions and going over with the thinning shears to neaten it up. **(2)**

If you are looking to give your dog a bell-shaped face, the length of hair on the chin should match the ears. Use the Adam's apple as a point of reference to set the bottom line of the bell shape.

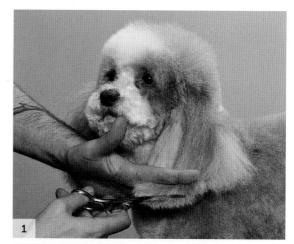

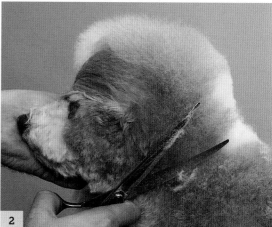

Short Ear Variations

If your dog's ears fold in half when he pays attention, shaving the bottom half of the ear gives them a supercute look and keeps the ears ventilated. This is especially good for dogs with ear problems.

Before

Start by placing the ear flap in your hand. Carefully clip the hair using a #10 blade, a #8½ blade, or a short attachment comb in the direction the hair grows. **(1)** Be constantly aware of where the edges of the ear flaps are to avoid cutting them. Holding the ear flap between your fingers and using your fingers as a guide, trim the edges from the base of the ear to the tip on the back part of the ears and then only the bottom half on the front part of the ears. **(2)** The hair left on the top half of the front will add some weight to the ears to keep them in place and will help to create a nice round face.

While pulling the ear forward, blend the head into the neck with the help of thinning shears. **(3)**

Using the same pattern but changing the lengths and angles will give you very different looks, allowing your creativity to flow.

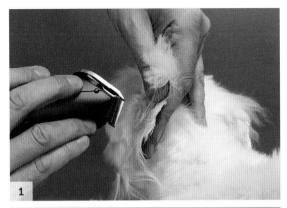

After

Clean Face

TOOLS NEEDED:

Clippers
#10 blade

A clean or shaved face could give any dog with a hairy face a unique and edgy look, not to mention the added practical benefits for dogs with medical issues. Not having a fuzzy face on dogs that suffer from excessive drool because of missing teeth, for example, will eliminate a potential bacteria haven that can easily get infected and will also make it much easier to keep them clean and dry.

When clipping a dog's face, it is crucial to be aware of the shape of your dog's bone structure around the eyes, lips, and folds of the skin, as well as the areas where the lack of fat makes the skin lie right on top of the bone. Dogs come in many different shapes and sizes, with many variations within their particular breed. In other words, you need to carefully go over their face and locate protruding bones and edges where the clipper could scratch and hurt the skin.

As a general rule, clippers must be handled with caution. This is even more important when they are being used to clip a dog's face. If your dog hasn't had his face shaved before, using a #10 blade is generally the safest way to go.

Maintaining a firm grip on your dog, but in a way that he will still feel comfortable, will help keep him calm during the clipping.

Slowly approach the dog with the clippers turned on to let him get used to the noise and vibration. Touching him with the back of the clipper is a good way to show your dog that everything is okay.

The hair on the face should be clipped against the grain. Holding his ears back will give you good visibility and will keep the skin taut, making it easier to clip.

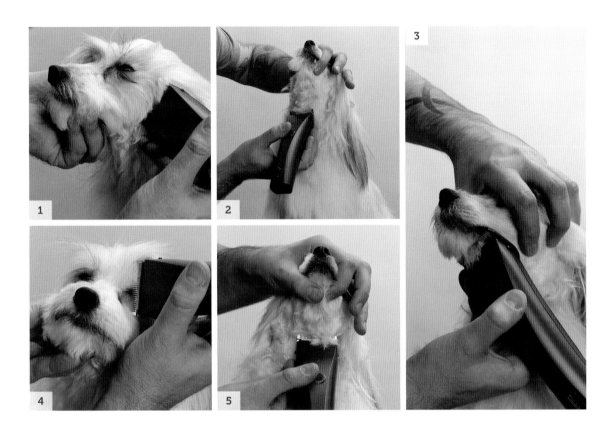

Start by clipping in a straight line from the base of the ear to the outside corner of his mouth. Then gently pull the skin back and proceed to carefully shave the side of the muzzle moving forward in the direction of the nose. **(1)**

As when handling other grooming tools around the eyes, always point them outward and away from the eyes to avoid any accidents.

The chin usually has a lot of folds and creases or wrinkles, so stretch them out with your fingers while shaving from the chin to the Adam's apple. Follow the direction of the hair growth or go against the growth for a shorter clip. (If the skin is not accustomed to being shaved, avoid going against the grain.) Be aware of any cowlicks on the dog's neck and try to position the clippers following the direction of the hair. **(2)** I find that using just one corner of the blade will give you more control when trimming the area near the lips. **(3)**

Follow this same method to clip the bridge of the nose, starting in between the eyes and then moving forward to the nose. **(4)**

Holding the dog's mouth closed will prevent the tongue from sticking out, or will at least make you aware of when it is about to happen. **(5)**

A good trick to keep the dog calm and quiet is to blow on him very gently, almost like a whisper. This will make him focus on that for a few precious seconds so you can execute your cuts.

Talking to your dog at this stage is counterproductive. You want to be quiet, soothing, and calm.

Bearded Face and Mohawk

TOOLS NEEDED:

Clippers

#10 blade

optional, #15, #30

Thinning shears

Hair spray

A bearded look, like those of a schnauzer, a wheaton terrier, or a Brussels griffon, will give the dog a very sharp and serious face. It is a very popular face, but obviously all that hair on the beard will require on-going attention because it will constantly be in the water bowl, in the food, and dragged over anything that the dog decides to sniff while out for a walk.

For added personality, follow these steps to achieve a bearded look with a retro Mohawk. You will have a sharp look in no time.

Using a #10 blade on your clippers and following the direction of the hair growth, clip the side of the head from the outside line where the Mohawk starts (usually a line between the top corner at the base of the ear to the inside corner of the eye), leaving the eyebrows. **(1)** Clip the cheeks from the outside corner of the eye to ¼ inch (6 mm) from the back corner of the mouth. **(2)**

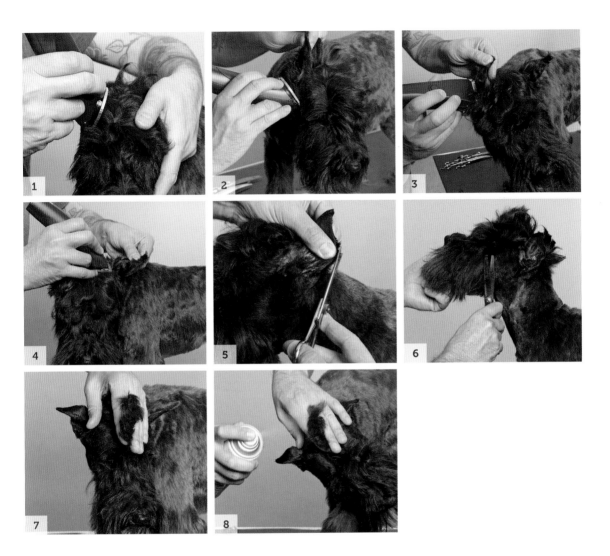

With the flap of the ear resting in the palm of your hand, clip the inside of the ear with a #10, #15, or #30 blade. **(3)** Clip the back and outside of the ear with a #10 or #15 blade. **(4)** Pulling the ear forward will give you a good visual of the back of the ear.

Trim around the ear flap using your fingers as a guide to avoid cutting the leather of the ear. **(5)**

With the help of thinning shears, blend the beard with the cheeks. **(6)**

Trim the eyebrows, pointing the thinning shears from the outside corner of the eye to the tip of the nose. With thinning shears, clean the area between the eyes and round off the eyebrows to give the dog a softer look. **(7)** Hold the Mohawk hair between your fingers and apply a little hair spray to make it stand up. **(8)**

With the thinning shears, trim the top of the Mohawk to give it a rounded shape that will blend into the neck. Finish the face by trimming the beard with thinning shears.

Clip Down

TOOLS NEEDED:

Slicker brush

Comb

Clippers

#10 blade for sanitary area

Blades #4, #5, #7F, and #8½ for the body, depending on the desired length

Straight shears

Curved scissors

Thinning shears

Clipping down a dog is not a decision based solely on style and aesthetics. Often, dogs with severe skin issues and that require frequent medicated baths will benefit from a very short haircut. In tropical areas, for example, where flea infestations can happen often and can be hard to control, maintaining a dog's hair clipped very short will make it easier to keep a close eye on bugs and avoid a few of them from turning into a huge infestation.

Be aware that clipping down a double-coated dog may affect the hair growth cycle.

To clip the dog, follow the direction of the hair growth, as shown in the image. **(1)**

Be sure to keep skin taut by gently pulling it with your free hand, paying close attention to avoid scratching folds, nipples, or growths. **(2)**

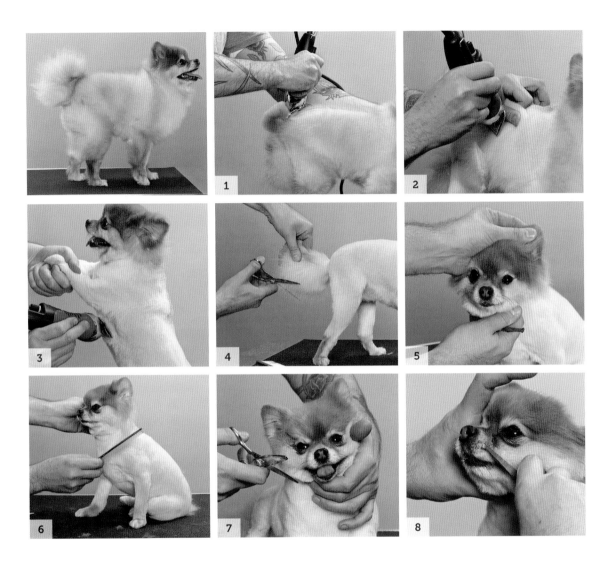

Also make sure you have a clear view while trimming the stomach to avoid scratching or cutting the delicate skin. **(3)**

Trim the tail with thinning shears. **(4)** Trim the head with thinning shears to blend it with the rest of the body.

When trimming around the ears, use your thumb as a guide to protect the edges of the ears. **(5)**

Comb the hair in different directions and go over it again with thinning shears to achieve a neat finish. **(6, 7)** Trim the whiskers with a small pair of round-tip scissors. **(8)**

Topknot

TOOLS NEEDED:

Small pillow or plush toy

Rat-tail comb

Rubber band

optional, rice paper

It is wise to remember that the primary purpose of a topknot on a dog is to keep the hair out of his eyes, not to give him an anesthesia-free facelift. To avoid this look, here are a few guidelines to help you create a beautiful crown of hair on top of your dog's head.

Start by making sure the dog is comfortable in the grooming area. Giving your dog an ear rub and a few minutes to relax will probably help to position him lying on his stomach. A small pillow or one of his favorite plush toys could help keep him comfortable.

Once he is resting in the correct position, use a rat-tail comb to divide the hair. Trace a line between the inside corners of the eyes, then comb the hair up and temporarily secure it with a hair clip on top of the head while you work on pulling up the hair from the sides. **(1)**

Trace a line with the rat-tail comb from the outside corner of one eye to the inside corner at the base of the ear, then repeat this procedure on the other side of the face. Be careful not to pull hair from the ear flap to avoid restricting the natural movement of the ear, which will cause discomfort to the dog and will make him try to "fix" it himself pulling the ponytail out. **(2)**

Finish separating the hair by tracing a semicircle at the back of the head. **(3)**

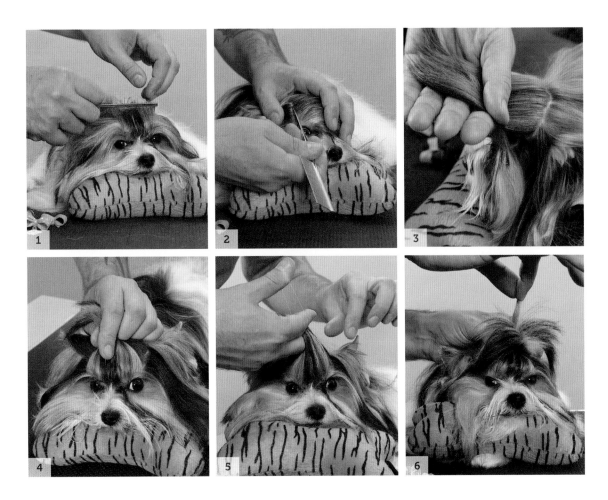

All the sides you traced should now form a circle, and at the center of this circle is where the ponytail should rest gently, held by the even support of a neat crown of hair. **(4)**

Holding the ponytail with one hand, secure it with a rubber band. **(5)** Gently pull the rubber band to the back to release some of the hair from the front. Move the ponytail back to the center and, pulling a few hairs from the center of the ponytail, secure it again in the desired position. **(6)** This will create a small puff, which will give the face a sweet expression.

With the help of the rat-tail comb, while holding the ponytail up, neaten the general appearance.

Putting a ponytail on your dog not only makes him look fabulous but also serves a practical purpose by keeping hair away from his eyes.

Keep in mind that rubber bands, when left in for too long, will break the hair. For an everyday hairdo, wrap the ponytail with a small square of rice paper before securing it with a rubber band to prevent hair damage.

Utility Cut

TOOLS NEEDED:

Clippers

#10 blade

#30 blade for attachment combs

#5, #7F, and #8½ blades for the body

Medium and short attachment combs for the legs and head

Slicker brush

Comb

Straight shears

Curved shears

Thinning shears

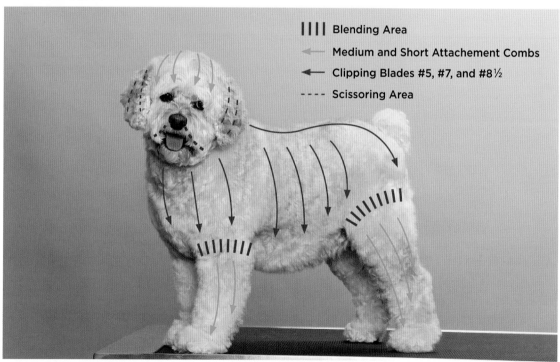

|||| Blending Area

Medium and Short Attachement Combs

Clipping Blades #5, #7, and #8½

---- Scissoring Area

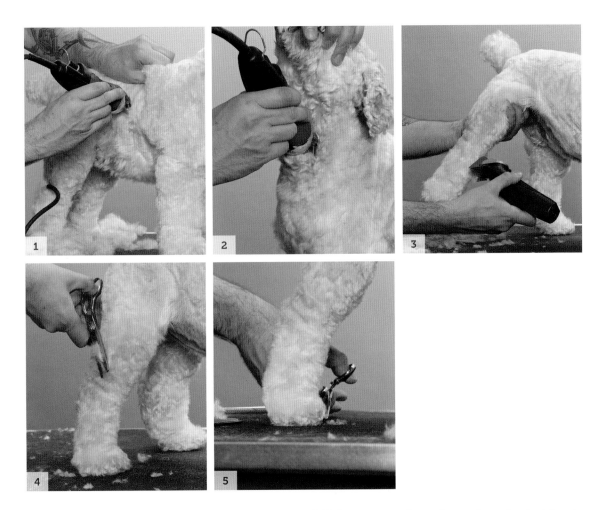

As stated by the name, this is a very practical cut that is especially popular during the warmer months. Keeping the hair on the body short with just some fluff in the legs will turn any high-maintenance coat into a style that is much easier to maintain.

Referring to the guidelines pictured, clip the body following the direction of the hair growth. Be sure to keep skin taut by gently pulling it with your free hand, paying close attention to avoid scratching folds, nipples, or growths. **(1)**

While trimming the neck area, keep the dog's head up to stretch the extra skin. **(2)**

With the medium attachment comb, clip the hair on the legs, combing the hair up and going over it again with the clippers and attachment comb to help achieve a smooth finish. **(3)**

Neaten the edges with the straight shears and blend with thinning shears. **(4)** Trim around the feet. **(5)**

(Continued)

Utility Cut (Continued)

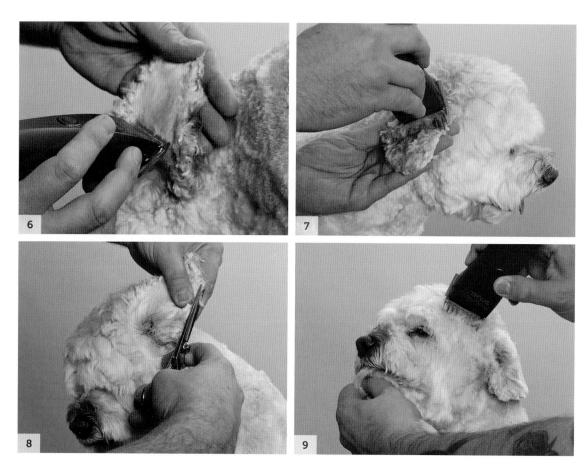

While resting the ear flap in the palm of your hand, shave the inside of the flap with a #10 blade, paying close attention to the edges. **(6)**

Using the clippers with the small attachment comb, trim the outside of the ear flaps in the direction of the hair growth. **(7)**

Trim the edges of the ear flaps with scissors using your fingers as a guide to avoid cutting the ear leather. **(8)**

Folding the ear flap back, clip down the side of the head with the short or medium attachment comb. **(9)**

With the help of thinning shears, trim the hair from the base of the ear to the outside corner of the eye. Trim the eyebrows with the thinning shears, pointing them from the outside corner of the eye to the nose and then across, to neaten the bangs. **(10)**

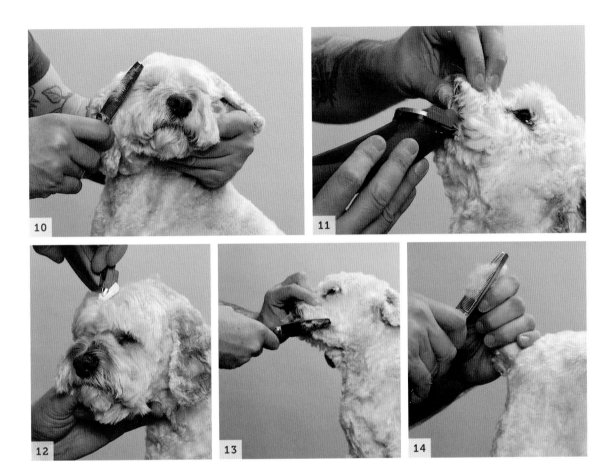

Holding up the dog's chin, with the short attachment comb, clip from the snout to the Adam's apple. **(11)**

Comb the hair on top of the head forward and go over, from the occiput to the eyebrows, with the short or medium attachment comb over the #30 blade on the clippers. **(12)**

Holding the dog's mouth closed, trim the sides of the muzzle with thinning shears. You may need to stop a few times while doing this because most dogs don't like to hold their mouths closed for too long. **(13)**

Trim the tail with scissors, finishing them with thinning shears. **(14)**

Scissor Cut

TOOLS NEEDED:

Clippers for pads and privates

Comb

Wide-tooth comb

Straight shears

Curved shears

Thinning shears

Finishing spray

When deciding on a hairstyle, nothing gives you more freedom than doing a whole grooming with scissors. However, keep in mind that it is the most labor-intensive of all the grooming techniques.

After the dog is washed and brushed, start trimming the pads and private areas using the clippers.

Start by combing the hair up away from the skin using a wide-tooth comb.

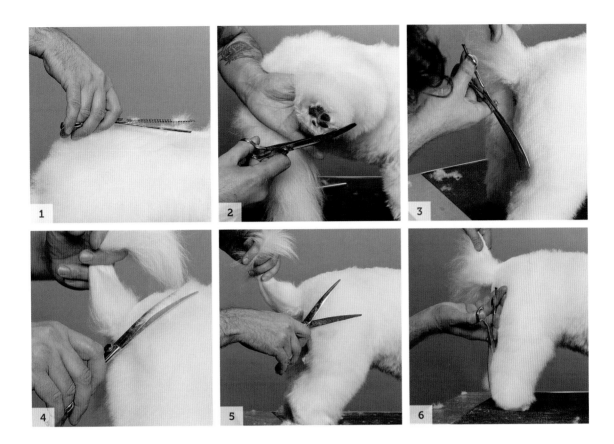

Back

Standing behind the dog, start setting up the topline using the floor as a reference to achieve a straight line. This is when you get to visually correct a faulty topline and provide a good reference point. **(1)**

Once the topline is set, trim around the feet to give you a reference of how much hair to leave when connecting the reference points.

Start by gently lifting the paw and trimming around with curved shears, keeping a 45-degree angle to create a nice beveled look. **(2)**

Comb the hair back on the back legs and, using the curved shears in an inverted position, start setting the back angulation. Use the bending point on the back of the leg as the shorter point of reference of the angulation, and the front part of the knee as the longest point when trimming the front of the back legs. **(3)**

Using the curved and straight shears, connect the topline, **(4)** back leg angulation, **(5)** and feet. **(6)**

Now it is time to move to the front.

(Continued)

Scissor Cut (Continued)

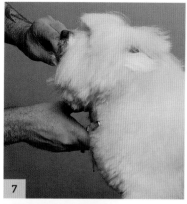

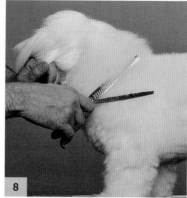

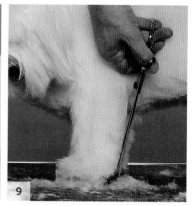

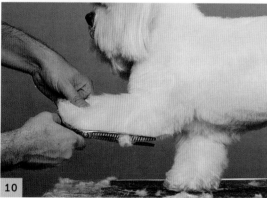

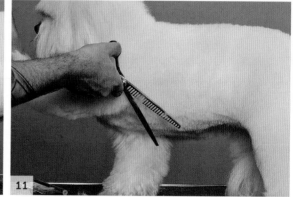

Front

Locate the dog's Adam's apple and start trimming from there to the point where the front leg meets the chest. This should be a soft curve that, when looked at from the profile, will smoothly connect the bottom of the chest with the rest of the dog's outline. **(7)**

Now connect the chest, neck, and side of the body using the shears that you feel most comfortable using. Follow the natural lines of the body. **(8)**

With the dog standing in a natural position, trim the front legs, combing the hair in different directions to be sure all hairs are trimmed to the desired length. **(9)**

Lift the front leg forward and comb the hair down to help you trim the back of each front leg. **(10)**

Finish trimming the body by going over with thinning shears to erase scissor marks. **(11)**

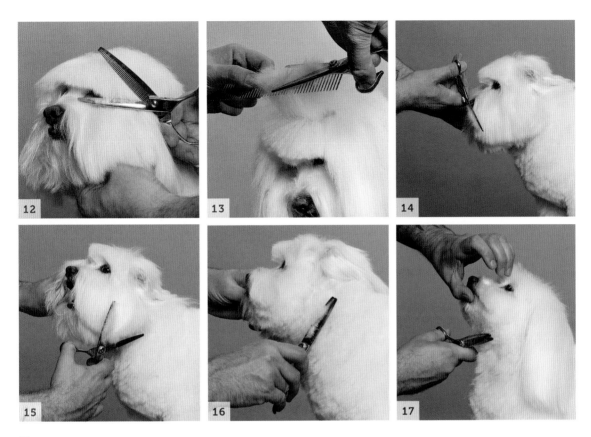

Face

To trim the face, start by combing all the hair from the top of the head forward.

With thinning shears, trim the hair from the outside corner of the eye with the scissors pointing toward the center of the nose. **(12)**

Repeat on the other side of the face and then round up the front of the visor.

Lifting the hair from the top of the head with a comb, start trimming the edges, little by little, combing the hair down and up again to achieve a smooth, natural layered look. **(13)**

Trim the sides of the head by connecting the tip of the nose with the base of the ear, creating a half-moon shape following the jawline.

Using thinning shears will let you create and correct the curve slowly without leaving sharp scissor marks. **(14)**

Use the comb to lift the sides of the face and trim the hair that sticks out of the imaginary line. Go over this area a few times with thinning shears to be sure you get a natural look. **(15)**

Keeping the ear flap over the head, blend the side of the head with the neck. **(16)**

Lifting the dog's chin up, trim the hair to smoothly connect the ear with the Adam's apple. **(17)**

Trim the hair on the ears to the desired length. Accessorize and you are ready to go!

Hand-stripping

Hand-stripping is a grooming technique used mostly on terriers, in which the dead coat is pulled from the roots instead of being clipped or cut. This technique allows the new hair to grow strong and thick with a harsher texture and helps the coat keep its original bright color. The benefit of hand-stripping a wiry coat is that the follicles will maintain their natural strength, texture, and integrity, which in turn will keep the coat practically odor-free for an extended period of time. When a wiry coat gets clipped, the hair can lose its natural texture and bright color, turning a wiry coat into a softer coat, which requires the dog to be groomed more often.

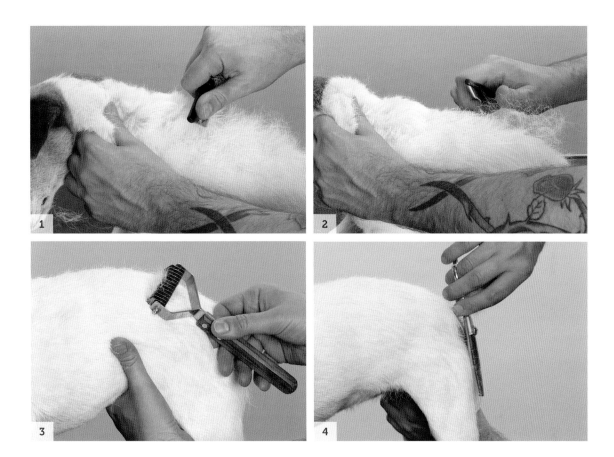

Hold the skin taut with one hand and with the other hand, grab a very small amount of hair between your thumb and the stripping knife. **(1)** Without twisting your wrist, pull the hair in the direction the hair is growing. Repeat this procedure in a systematic way, section by section, going from the top of the neck to the tail. **(2)** For dogs with thick undercoats, the use of an undercoat rake can make the job easier by speeding up the process. **(3)**

It is better to do hand-stripping when the dog is dirty because the hair is less slippery. After the procedure is done, you should bathe the dog using a soothing naturally medicated shampoo to prevent itching.

Running the stripping knife flat over the coat will help to achieve a flat look. While trimming the face, pull only two or three hairs at a time, always in the direction of hair growth. Finish the grooming by going over the outline with thinning shears. **(4)**

Puppy Cut

TOOLS NEEDED:

Clippers

#7F blade for the body

#10 blade for the sanitary clip

#30 blade for the pads

Medium (1-inch [2.5 cm]) snap-on attachment comb for the head

Thinning shears for blending

Straight shears for the outline

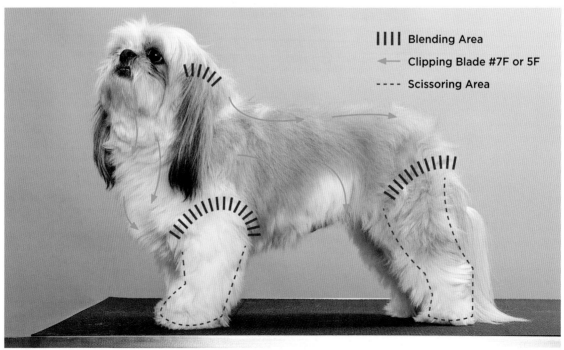

|||| Blending Area

← Clipping Blade #7F or 5F

---- Scissoring Area

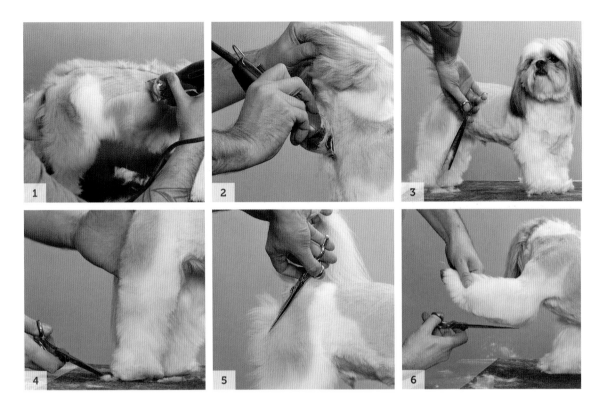

This haircut is very popular because it is low maintenance and can be both glamorous and practical.

This same cut can be used year-round by changing the length of the hair left on the body using a different blade or snap-on comb. It is also the perfect haircut for the "fashionista" who loves to wear clothes: It prevents the hair from getting matted and allows the clothes to fit better.

Start by trimming the sanitary and eye areas (refer to these sections on pages 82 and 88). Then, clip the dog's body from the top of the neck to the base of the tail and down to the sides of the body. **(1)**

To trim the neck area, locate the Adam's apple and clip down following the direction the hair grows. Be aware of any cowlicks and pay close attention to the neck area, which has many folds and wrinkles. Remember to use your free hand to hold the skin taut while clipping these areas. **(2)**

Before trimming the back legs, it is important to identify the bending points of the legs (backs and fronts of the knees). Cutting the hair shorter at the back of the knee and leaving it longer at the front will visually accentuate the dog's natural angulation and make him look more elegant. **(3)**

To trim the legs, trim around the feet, positioning the scissors at a 45-degree angle to give the feet a beveled effect. **(4)** Then blend the hair from the legs by combing the hair out and keeping the scissors perpendicular to the floor, trim the hair to the desired length. **(5)** Be aware that not all dogs have straight legs. Enhancing the indentations by leaving more hair will make the legs visually straight. Pull the leg forward and trim the excess hair. **(6)**

Go over your work with thinning shears to create a smooth finish.

Teddy Bear Cut

TOOLS NEEDED:

Clippers

Medium or large attachment comb for the body

#10 blade for the sanitary clip

#30 blade for the attachment combs

Slicker brush

Thinning shears

Straight shears

Curved shears

Comb

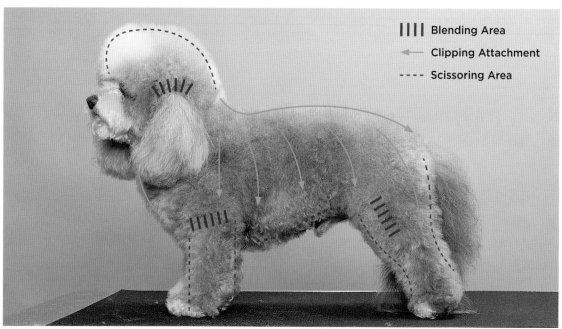

|||| Blending Area

← Clipping Attachment

---- Scissoring Area

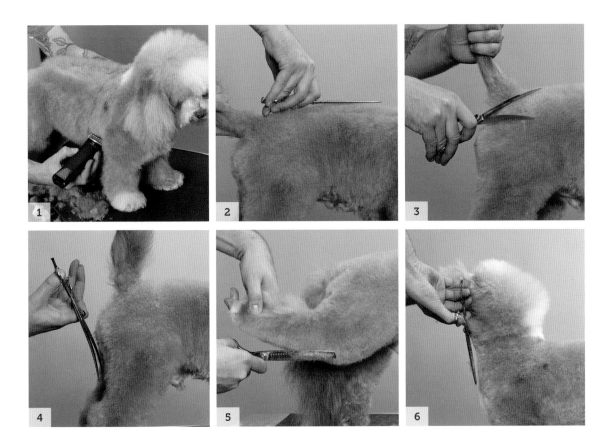

This haircut, as the name indicates, reminds us of the classic, fluffy, stuffed toy featuring soft, rounded edges and a sweet and cuddly look.

Using the clippers with a medium or large attachment comb over a #30 blade, clip the body following the direction of the hair growth. **(1)**

With the dog standing in his natural position, use the straight shears to trim the topline, holding the shears parallel to the floor to achieve a straight and level cut. **(2)**

Keeping the dog's tail up, use the curved shears to start blending the topline to the side of the legs, keeping the shears perpendicular to the floor to achieve a straight-looking leg. **(3)**

With the same curved shears, follow the angulation of the back legs, using the bending points on the back of the knee as a point of reference to mark the shortest point and the front of the knee as the point where you will leave the longest hair when accentuating the curve. **(4)**

Gently lift the back leg, comb the hair down, and trim the front of the back leg, smoothly connecting the outline of the leg with the rest of the body. **(5)**

Trim the head referring to the guidelines pictured. Go over all of your work with thinning shears to erase any marks left by the clippers or scissors. **(6)**

Poodle Cut

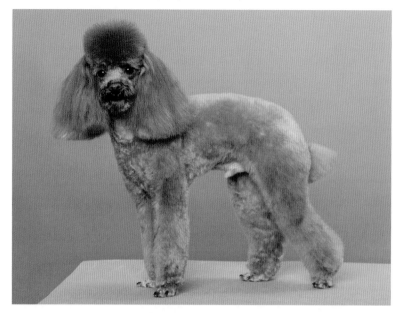

TOOLS NEEDED:

Clippers

#10 blade for the sanitary area, face, and paws

#4 blade for the body

Medium or large attachment comb

#30 blade for the attachment combs

Curved scissors

Slicker brush

Comb

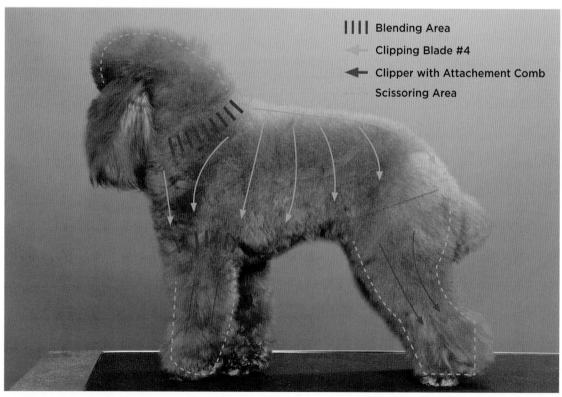

|||| Blending Area

← Clipping Blade #4

← Clipper with Attachement Comb

Scissoring Area

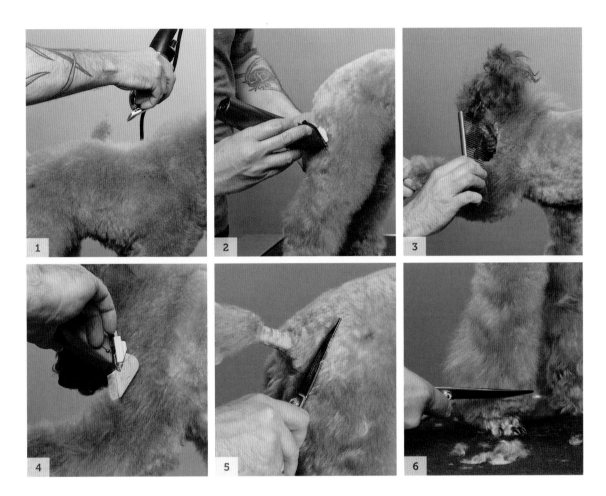

Body

Probably the most iconic dog where grooming is concerned, a poodle can be trimmed in a large variety of cuts. Here are the step-by-step directions for a simple but still poodle-like cut.

Referring to the guidelines pictured, clip the back and body using a #4 blade on the clippers, following the direction of the hair growth. **(1)**

Trim the legs using a medium or large attachment comb, following the direction of the hair growth. Brush or comb the hair up and go over with the clippers again to be sure all the hair is the same length. **(2)**

Pulling the front leg forward, gently comb the hair up and go over with the attachment comb. Comb again and repeat. **(3, 4)**

With curved shears, blend the legs into the body. **(5)**

Trim the bottom of the leg with curved scissors at a 45-degree angle to achieve a nice beveled finish. **(6)**

(Continued)

Poodle Cut (Continued)

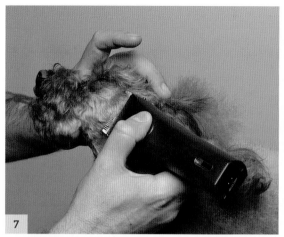

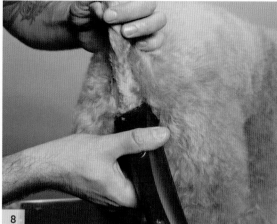

Head & Tail

Referring to the guidelines pictured, shave with a #10 or #15 blade from the base of the ear to the inside corner of the eye and down to the outside corner of the mouth. **(7)**

Be extra careful when trimming the hair from the lower eyelid. This is one of the few times that you should go against the grain. Trim the neck from the base of the ear to the Adam's apple and up to the neck, leaving hair on the chin.

Shave the base of the tail with a #10 or #15 blade. **(8)**

With the curved shears, blend the front of the neck with the rest of the body and finish with thinning shears to erase any scissor marks. **(9)**

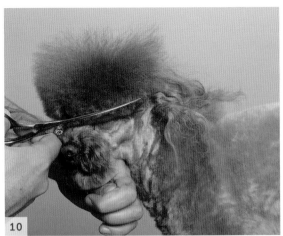

Blend the sides of the head with the top using curved shears at a 45-degree angle. **(10)**

Comb the hair on top of the head to one side and with the curved shears, trim anything that goes over the top of the ear. Repeat this process on the other side. **(11)**

Comb the hair on top forward and with curved shears, trim the hair to form a semicircle that connects both tops of the ears. **(12)**

(Continued)

Poodle Cut (Continued)

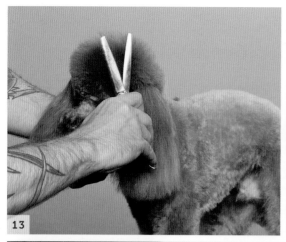

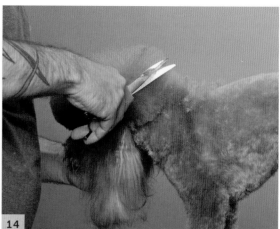

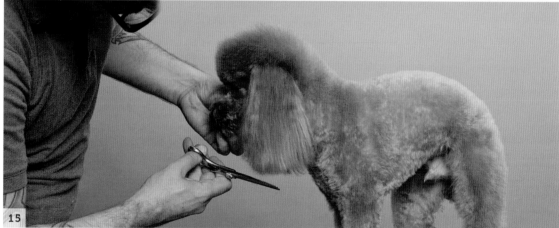

Go over the entire head with thinning shears to give it a softer look and erase scissor marks. **(13)**

With curved shears, blend the back of the head with the neck. **(14)**

Comb the ears down and trim the bottom of each ear. **(15)**

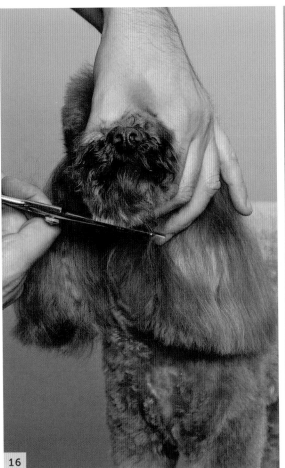

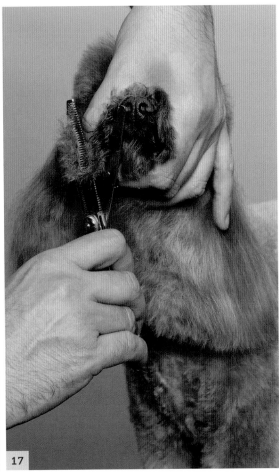

Comb the hair of the mustache forward and, holding the muzzle with your hand, trim around the muzzle to give it a rounded look. **(16)**

Finish with thinning shears, blending into the back of the muzzle. **(17)** Use your fingers as a guide to trim the hair by and around the lips to avoid getting too close and accidentally cutting your dog's tongue.

CHAPTER 6

Solutions to Common Problems

There is nothing we love more than to watch our dogs running free and burning off all that pent-up energy, but sometimes those fun and wild runs, or even things that happen during regular walks around the block, can end up in a grooming disaster when we realize that our pooch has stepped into or run through something sticky or messy.

The effectiveness of the following solutions will depend on the kind of hair your dog has. Harsher coats usually will be easier to clean up because the hair is stronger and typically its structure will naturally repel a lot of the most common substances, keeping them on the surface. On double-coated dogs, any substance that gets in contact will penetrate the soft undercoat, making it a little more difficult to remove the substance and often calling for a second round of the designated cleaning process.

Here are some of the most common problems.

Grease

You must act as fast as you can to remove grease because it could spread all over the dog pretty quickly, and if your dog decides to groom himself, licking the substances could be toxic.

First, apply a generous amount of cornstarch and massage the stain to make sure that most of the grease gets absorbed. After a couple of minutes, brush the powder off, preferably with an old slicker brush or one that you can wash. You don't want to have the brush you regularly use impregnated with grease. Proceed to wash his paws or the affected areas with a degreasing shampoo or a small amount of dishwashing liquid. Let the shampoo sit for a couple of minutes and then rinse off thoroughly. Repeat if necessary. Using a washcloth could also help remove the oil. Dry the affected area and then apply a small amount of cornstarch or baby powder to be sure that any oily residue gets absorbed.

Dirt and Mud

If your dog had too much fun running through puddles of mud and you don't have a tub handy to give him a bath, the best solution is to let him dry and then, after sprinkling some cornstarch over the dirty areas, brush off the mud with the help of a slicker brush.

Gum

Not only is it horrifying to find a piece of gum in our dog's hair, but to think where it was before is even more horrifying. Thankfully, removing the gum is not as hard as it seems.

One easy solution is to impregnate the gum with peanut butter. Work it in well with your fingers to allow the oil to break apart the gum. After a couple of minutes, use a comb to start opening the gum from the outside first while still working in more of the peanut butter. Don't worry about sticky fingers—I'm sure your dog will be happy to help with that.

Keeping your dog's paws well trimmed is the best way to prevent gum from sticking to your dog's pads.

Paint

Water-based paints are not hard to remove. If it has already dried, use a slicker brush to get rid of as much paint as possible to break the "seal." Follow by soaking a washcloth with shampoo (if it doesn't work, use some dish detergent). Follow by rinsing the area well.

Oil paint can be a bit more difficult to remove. Soak the stain with vegetable oil, let it sit overnight, and then proceed to remove the paint with a washcloth soaked in dish detergent. Rinse well. If the painted spot is on an area where the dog can lick it, cover it with a t-shirt or a bandage. Sometimes, depending on the temperament of your dog, it is a good idea to use an E-collar to prevent him from reaching the affected area.

Candle Wax

The first step should be to check to make sure that the hot wax hasn't reached and burned the skin.

Start by removing as much of the wax as you can with the end of a comb and working it with your fingers to crack it as much as possible. Add some peanut butter, vegetable oil, or mineral oil on the affected area and after working it with your fingers, use the comb to help the wax slip off. Never apply heat to melt the wax because it could easily burn the dog. Wash the area and rinse well.

Superglue

As implied by the name, superglue is not easy to remove. Like gum, trying to loosen it with vegetable or mineral oil could work. Let it sit for a few minutes and then use a comb to try to remove it, working on a small portion at a time.

If this doesn't work and the glue mess is superficial enough, carefully trimming the hair could be the only option. Carefully slide a comb under the glue and without pulling, so as not to hurt the dog, with a small pair of round-tip scissors, cut the portion of hair affected halfway. With your fingers, open up the hair and repeat the oil process. Use a washcloth soaked in dishwashing liquid and work it with your fingers. Rinse well.

Skunk

There are 1,001 opinions on how best to remove skunk smell from your dog. First, it is important to understand exactly what this agent is and what it is made of. The substance that a skunk sprays is an oily secretion, generated from glands under the skunk's tail, whose basic chemical compound is called thiol. Thiol is a resistant substance that bonds with proteins, which is why it will remain even after washing. Similar compounds are found in onions and in garlic, which is why their smell also lingers after washing our hands. Tomato juice will only mask the smell. To neutralize the skunk's secretions, use a mixture of 1 quart (945 ml) 3 percent hydrogen peroxide and ¼ cup (55 g) baking soda. Add a little liquid detergent to this mix.

Remember that the skunk will most likely spray your dog when he is approaching him, so the biggest concentration will be on your dog's face. Using a washcloth soaked in the peroxide solution will allow you to get to every little corner of your dog's face.

Fleas and Ticks

There are literally hundreds of types of fleas and ticks, but one characteristic they all share is trouble. Fleas and ticks are a serious problem that, if left unattended, can lead to a whole host of problems. The consensus is that preventing a flea and tick problem is better than treating one.

Always inspect your dog for any type of flea or tick (or both) and address any problem immediately if found. White dogs with short coats tend to be the easiest breeds to inspect. Dogs with longer and darker coats logically require a more thorough inspection. Here is where a properly executed line-brushing is indispensable because it will help you visually inspect your dog section by section down to the skin.

Frequent bathing is essential, especially for dogs that frequently spend time outdoors. Using a shampoo with strong-scented natural oils such as eucalyptus or tea tree oil might help repel fleas if your dog comes into contact with them. Frequently vacuum your home, especially your furniture and rugs. Many dogs sleep in our beds, so remember to wash your sheets frequently and to use a mattress cover.

Be proactive rather than reactive and both you and your dog will benefit.

You can also use preventive flea and tick topical medications recommended by your veterinarian. These are especially helpful in the Southern United States, where the flea and tick problem is more serious.

Follow the manufacturer's directions when using medicated flea and tick shampoos because any medicated shampoo, including flea and tick products, left on the dog longer than directed could seriously irritate the skin.

When using medicated shampoos or any product that will sit on the dog for an extended period of time, it is important to apply eye-protecting drops to avoid any of the products from dripping into the eyes.

Have a clean washcloth handy to wipe away any products from delicate areas. The genital and perianal areas are especially sensitive.

Take into consideration that some natural flea and tick products are not strong enough to kill flea eggs, so repeating the treatment a few days later will help to finish the job.

The type of flea will vary depending on where you live. Fortunately, they can all be treated the same way. Make sure to keep your backyard clean and the grass mowed. Fleas tend to thrive in high grass and weeds and in shaded, moist areas. Keeping your yard free of leaves and the grass cut, so that the hot sun has the opportunity to heat and dry your backyard, will help remove breeding areas.

When a flea bites a dog, it leaves behind its saliva. Many dogs are extremely sensitive to the flea saliva and can immediately develop allergy symptoms. It only takes a single flea bite to throw a dog with sensitive skin into an itching spell that will require immediate veterinary attention to stop him from hurting himself, which he will do by frantically biting and scratching his skin to try to stop the burning and itching.

Ticks, on the other hand, rarely cause an immediate reaction, which is why they can go undetected much longer, exposing your dog and even yourself to sometimes life-threatening problems. Ticks can transmit more than a dozen diseases, including Lyme disease, Rocky Mountain spotted fever, and tularemia, among others.

Flea and tick products cover a wide spectrum of tick species, but not all of them. Because no one product on the market can kill all the varieties, it is important to be able to identify ticks to know what kind of transmitted disease your dog has been exposed to.

Removing Fleas

Running a flea comb over your dog is the best way to remove the fleas. Depending on the type of coat, you can do this while the dog is still wet or after he has been dried. A plastic flea comb is safe to use around the face due to its flexibility.

Removing Ticks

After choosing the right tool to remove the tick, fill a small container with rubbing alcohol to deposit and kill the ticks that you have already taken off your pet. Flushing ticks won't kill them. (I'm not 100 percent sure they won't find their way back home, so why not just get rid of them once and for all?)

Wear gloves because a tick's saliva carries diseases that are transmittable to humans. With a pair of tweezers or a special tick removal tool, gently grab the tick as close to the skin as you can and with a slow but steady motion, pull the tick up. After you have removed the tick, clean the area with rubbing alcohol and add a small amount of antibiotic ointment.

If any piece of the tick's head was left inside the skin, the dog's natural body response will be to create a small welt on the bite spot. Keep an eye on the welt, but most likely it will disappear in a few days.

If you live in an area where ticks are known for carrying diseases, it is a good idea to save the evidence in case you need to show it to the vet.

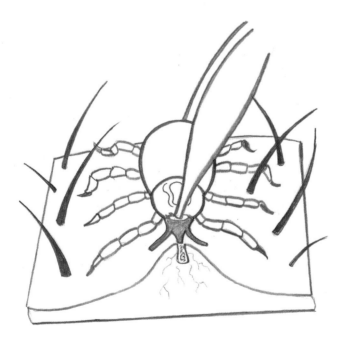

First Aid

When it comes to your pet's first aid, an ounce of prevention is worth a pound of cure.

Just like us, when a dog gets hurt he could easily become agitated, angry, and scared, and all the "he will never jump," "he will never bite," or "he will never run" can easily change when the dog is under stress or pain. Reacting quickly will help neutralize a bad situation and avoid making the problem worse. Every grooming kit should have a basic dog first-aid kit for grooming-related injuries.

Knowledge is power. Knowing some basic first-aid procedures will help you react calmly and with confidence, keeping your dog calm as well. First aid is exactly that—first aid. Its objective is to relieve a dog from pain and discomfort, but it should be followed by a call to your veterinarian to assess if further treatment is necessary.

Never leave your dog unattended in the grooming area, whether it's a grooming table or a countertop. Unattended dogs may jump off the grooming area and hurt themselves.

While blow-drying your dog, make sure they are calm and in a ventilated area to avoid overheating. Dog skin is very sensitive and can burn easily. It is important to keep the hair dryer on the lowest heat setting and at a safe distance (about 15 inches [38.1 cm]) so as not to burn the skin. While bathing, sudden changes in water temperature can easily burn your dog's skin.

The most common grooming-related burns are those from hot water or hot air. These injuries can be divided into two categories.

First-Degree Burns

The skin will remain intact showing some redness and possible local inflammation.

Treat the area with a slow stream of cold water or hold a washcloth soaked in cold water on the area for a few minutes to be sure the skin's temperature drops. After the skin has cooled off, pat dry and apply some aloe vera gel. Avoid applying oils such as butter or ointments because they will keep the area hot instead of cooling it down. First-degree burns most likely can be treated at home without a vet visit, but if the symptoms don't go away it is important to contact your veterinarian because it could be an indication that deeper skin tissues have been affected.

Second-Degree Burns

These burns are more serious. The skin will show extreme redness and depending on the amount of exposure to the heat, blisters will appear. Second-degree burns need to be treated by a veterinarian as soon as possible. Cool the area with a clean, preferably sterile, cloth that won't leave lint on the wound. Keep rewetting the cloth to help reduce the temperature of the affected area and stop deeper tissue damage. Like with first-degree burns, do not apply any butter, oil, or ointment. Focus on keeping the area cold while you get the dog to the vet.

Clipping and Shaving Injuries

Skin injuries can also occur during clipping or shaving. Be careful when clipping or shaving dogs that have extremely matted coats because mats are usually very close to the skin. The closer your tools get to the skin, the more chances there will be for a cut or bruise.

In the case of a small cut, rinse the area to remove loose hair, pat dry, and apply a small amount of styptic powder to stop the bleeding. It is important to keep the dog calm.

Wrap the wound with clean gauze and contact your vet for further treatment. In the case of nipping the dog's tongue, apply pressure with a dry towel to control the bleeding. If the dog doesn't cooperate, run a slow stream of cold water on the injury to help constrict the blood vessels and slow down the bleeding.

Leg Injuries

If your dog jumps from the grooming area and hurts his leg, it is important, if you suspect that he has broken a bone, to immobilize the leg as soon as possible to avoid further injury. Using the inner cardboard tube of a paper towel roll as a "cast" could help keep the leg immobilized until you get to the vet. Open the cardboard tube with scissors and after wrapping the injured leg with gauze, wrap the tube around the leg and secure it by wrapping it again to keep it in place.

If you can't hold the dog while making a phone call, place it in a small area to restrict as much of the dog's movement as possible.

CHAPTER 7

Grooming Solutions from Your Pantry

On more than one occasion I have run out of a grooming product and have had to figure out what I could use as a substitute to pet store products. Even though products specifically made for dogs are always the best option, when, for any reason they are not available, they can be replaced with certain household products.

Here is a list of some of the most common problems and how to take care of them by a visit to the pantry.

Alex Papachristidis, interior designer and author of The Age of Elegance and his Yorkie, Teddy. (www.alexpapachristidis.com)

Using Essential Oils

The benefits of aromatherapy and essential oils are widely known, and dogs can benefit from it as much as humans do.

Author Christine Wildwood writes in her book *Aromatherapy: Massage with Essential Oils:* "Essential oils promote natural healing by stimulating and reinforcing the body's own mechanisms. Essences of chamomile and thyme, for instance, are credited with the ability to stimulate the production of white blood cells which help in our fight against disease."

You can also learn a lot about essential oils and their benefits just by reading the ingredient lists on many pet shampoo bottles.

Here is a brief description of the effects attributed to some of the most common essential oils. Remember that essential oils must be diluted. Six to eight drops in a 6-ounce (175 ml) spray bottle with distilled water is a safe ratio.

Lavender Oil

This is probably the most commonly used of all essences, not only for its pleasant fragrance but also for its antifungal, anti-germicide, anti-anxiety, antidepressant, and calming properties. Rubbing a drop on your finger and massaging your dog's pads before a long trip or a grooming session can help him relax. I encourage you to spray some in the air for you to sniff while grooming your dog to reduce your anxiety as well.

Grapefruit Oil

Like most citrus oils, grapefruit oil is great during the summer as a natural bug repellant, especially in tick-infested areas. Misting your dog with a mix of grapefruit oil, tea tree oil, and lavender oil before going out is a great way to keep bugs away.

Peppermint Oil

Peppermint oil will not only turn a leave-in conditioner into the perfect holiday fragrance, but it is also a great scent to help with car sickness (you don't want your dog to get carsick on your way to an event).

Rosemary Oil

Rosemary oil is a great oil to help reduce itching. Mixing rosemary oil with lavender is a great natural option to help dogs with skin problems.

Dry Shampoo

I am sure that I am not the only one who, while getting ready to entertain friends at home, has suddenly realized that my dog is having a very bad hair day and that there is no time for a full grooming. It is at times like these that a dry shampoo can come in handy.

Dry Shampoo Mixture

To create your own dry shampoo, mix one part cornstarch with one part baby powder in a container with a lid then add a few drops of essential oils and some rice to keep the mix from forming lumps. Shake the mixture and then transfer it to a container with a perforated lid to be able to sprinkle it over the dog.

Place the dog over a towel or in an area that will be easy to clean after you brush out the powder from the dog's coat. Protect the dog's eyes from the powder with your hand and then sprinkle powder over the dog's coat, especially behind the ears where oils can easily accumulate. Let the powder sit for a minute and then brush out with a slicker brush.

Non-Rinse Solution

If you have a short-haired dog whose coat looks dull and dusty, a quick trick is to use a mixture of one part mouthwash with one part distilled water. Spray this onto the dog's coat to get rid of dandruff, dust, and extra oil. After spraying the mix all over the dog, taking care to avoid the eyes and mouth, run a dry washcloth over the dog's body to remove the excess solution, dust, and dandruff.

Leave-in Conditioner

Hair is elastic, so misting it with a leave-in conditioner before brushing will help to soften the hair and make it easier to run the brush through it. The homemade alternative is a solution of warm water (distilled water if you plan to store it for a while) and a few drops of hair conditioner made for humans.

For a slightly more sophisticated solution, mix 6 ounces (175 ml) of distilled water with 1 teaspoon of glycerin and up to six to eight drops of essential oils.

Paw Care

When the dog's pads get dry due to walking on hot surfaces or on winter salts, pet paw balms can be replaced by rubbing a few drops of olive oil on your fingers and massaging the oil into the dog's pads. If doing this indoors, be sure to pat-dry the pads before you let your dog jump on the couch.

Ear Cleaner

Ear cleaner can be replaced by mixing one part witch hazel with one part distilled white vinegar. If you don't have witch hazel, you can use rubbing alcohol. Note, however, that if the dog appears to have an active ear infection, either because the ear looks red and inflamed, has a strong smell, and/or the dog is shaking his head with discomfort, alcohol could sting and make the dog uncomfortable.

Organic coconut oil has been used by dog groomers and breeders for a long time to treat ear mites and yeast infections and to reduce swelling. The smooth texture is very soothing. One word of caution: When used on long-haired dogs, wipe off as much oil as you can after the application to avoid dripping on the coat. It is a good idea to start using it a couple of days before the bath, once a day, to soften up all the wax and debris, which will make cleanup easier on bath day.

The Lauren family likes a natural look for "Bikini", the family Yorkie. Author of *The Hamptons: Food, Family, and History* by Ricky Lauren (Wiley).

Dubbed the "architect of style" by Vogue's former style editor Billy Nowhich, David Monn is known for his meticulous attention to detail, including the care he takes of "Sammy", his beloved Cavalier King Charles Spaniel. (www.davidmonn. com)

CH. Morningstar Reverie

Best of Breed, The Pekingese Club of America National Specialty

Multiple Best in Show All Breed and Specialty Winner

Award of Merit Winner Westminster Kennel Club

Register of Merit Sire, The Pekingese Club of America

Photo courtesy of John D. French, breeder/owner, and Tony Rosato, co-breeder/owner

"Aside from being an utter professional and an absolute delight, Jorge makes our dog Joe look like a movie star!" – Phoebe Cates and Kevin Kline.

Photo by Heather Green

About the Author

Born in Buenos Aires, Argentina, Jorge Bendersky became interested in dogs at a very early age.

Known as a celebrity dog stylist and pet trendsetter, Jorge is a passionate educator with a strong belief that knowing how to properly groom your own dog will deepen the bond between a pet and his owner and help improve the pet's and the owner's quality of life.

With more than twenty years of experience working as a professional groomer in New York City, Jorge has developed a grooming and pet-care philosophy based on practicality but without the loss of glamour.

Behind the scenes, Jorge applies his passion for animals to improve the lives of all dogs, especially those in shelters and rescue situations. Through his tireless efforts and dedication, he has been honored with national humanitarian awards for his educational workshops for pet owners in the inner cities, for his volunteer efforts with animal rescues, and for his years of bringing attention to the importance of our responsibility to not only dogs but also all animals.

Visit www.planetjorge.com to find all the products you need to groom your dog and—why not—your friends' dogs too.

Index